THE NEGOTIATION COACH

Peter Fleming

The Teach Yourself series has been trusted around the world for over 60 years. It has helped millions of people to improve their skills and achieve their goals. This new 'Coach' series of business books is created especially for people who want to focus proactively on a specific workplace skill and to get a clear result at the end of it. Whereas many business books help you talk the talk, the Coach will help you walk the walk.

THE NEGOTIATION COACH

Peter Fleming

Teach Yourself®

First published in Great Britain in 2015 by John Murray Learning. An Hachette UK company.

This edition published in 2015 by John Murray Learning

British Library Cataloguing in Publication Data: a catalogue record for this title is available from the British Library.

Library of Congress Catalog Card Number: on file.

ISBN 978 1 473 60535 0

1

Typeset by Cenveo® Publisher Services.

Printed and bound in Great Britain by CPI Group (UK) Ltd., Croydon, CR0 4YY.

John Murray Learning policy is to use papers that are natural, renewable and recyclable products and made from wood grown in sustainable forests. The logging and manufacturing processes are expected to conform to the environmental regulations of the country of origin.

John Murray Learning
Carmelite House
50 Victoria Embankment
London
EC4Y 0DZ
www.hodder.co.uk

CONTENTS

MEET THE COACH

Peter Fleming is a Chartered Fellow of both the Chartered Institute of Marketing and also the Chartered Institute of Personnel Development – having been awarded an Oxford Master's in Human Resource Management. With significant retail experience in the UK (marketing and buying) and people development with a UK government agency, he established his own business consultancy group which provides structured learning projects in the UK, Europe and the Middle East.

This is his eighth published book and his fourth on this topic – but the first in the coaching format; it uses some of the proven techniques resulting from his pioneering research on improving the effectiveness of management learning.

'AS WE TEACH, SO WE LEARN…'

I would like to dedicate this book to the thousands of negotiators that I have worked with in our workshops (both in the UK and internationally), sharing learning experiences and a wide range of techniques – many of which are mentioned here. My work with top executives, marketing and procurement personnel – as well as with HR and staff representatives – has helped fashion the lifetime of experience that underpins this manual.

HOW TO USE THIS BOOK

This manual provides a powerful development method for anyone who feels the need to improve their negotiating skills. Unlike many books on this subject, this one focuses on collaborative bargaining (or 'win/win'). Some 'larger-than-life personalities' may use methods that are effective for them but less so for the rest of us; *The Negotiation Coach* offers a logical, step-by-step approach to negotiating explored through a series of practical coaching sessions that will develop your skills.

You may be preparing for an important forthcoming negotiation (that could make a major contribution to your own organizational objectives), or feel the need to overcome reservations about your own abilities to negotiate and reach an equitable result for both sides. Either way, this book is for you.

You might think that achieving a win/win result is easy (in contrast to win/lose – or even lose/lose) – but nothing could be further from the truth, especially in a highly competitive market or climate where negotiators are actively encouraged to believe that they must seek a win regardless of the effect on the other party. Coaching is a process that seeks to help negotiators *find their own solutions* to these dilemmas – and, therefore, achieve significantly greater success in their negotiations. By posing searching questions, the exercises throughout this book aim to replicate the self-analysis process and enable you to adopt more effective:

- objectives
- tools to achieve those objectives
- longer-term and more satisfactory results.

A real-life coach would be readily accessible, active and responsive. Here we are replicating that process by posing questions that may:

- provoke new responses that you did not have in your original negotiation plan
- help you identify alternative ways of tackling a negotiation project
- identify better ways of approaching negotiation projects (and negotiators) in the future.

Each chapter has the following features:

- **Outcomes from this chapter**   A list at the start of each chapter sets out exactly what you will have gained from that chapter by the time you have finished it. This is in terms of both what you will have *learned* (e.g. from the running text) and what you will have *completed* (e.g. in the coaching sessions).

- **Coaching sessions**   These are the learning tasks within each chapter that are designed to help you become a (better) negotiator. You will develop your skills by working through the tasks, which include the following activities:

  i. **Self-analysis** – designed to help you think about any negotiating you may have done in the past – even if it concerned household tasks within your family – and how you have felt about your successes or failures

  ii. **A review of those tasks** – as if you were talking to your coach across a desk or in your home – with the idea of setting goals for improvement

  iii. **Guidance on a topic** – to include skills used by successful negotiators, and some common 'traps' that might lead to unwelcome results or outcomes

  iv. **Your personal action plan** for future negotiations, based on your learning from the self-reflective exercises designed to get you thinking about this topic at a deeper level.

- **Coach's tips**   These are concise pieces of advice, often drawn from the author's own experience.

- **Case studies**   We will also explore negotiating through a series of linked scenarios which, though theoretical, are based on the author's experiences and illustrate how the skills can help (or hinder!) progress in real life. They illustrate both opportunities for improvement and/or use/misuse of the techniques described in the text (encouraging your own lateral thinking on opportunities for negotiating outcomes in your own field).

- **Next steps**   This section at the end of each chapter summarizes what you have learned and places that learning in the context of the chapters that follow.

- **Takeaways**   Some reflective questions at the end of each chapter will help you focus on what you have learned and how what you have read and carried out in that chapter has helped you, *personally*.

It is important to work through the practical exercises truthfully, realistically – with a personal commitment to improvement – and with sensitivity. Some of the techniques mentioned may sit comfortably with your own style, but even those that don't may give you cause to review your current methods and consider whether they might be holding you back. Please make the fullest use of the action plan in the appendix at the end of the book, adding notes to it as you work through the advice and guidance in each chapter.

The Negotiation Coach offers these key benefits:

1. A self-development text, enabling you to prepare and plan how to apply and test your new skills at your own pace

2. Opportunities for progressive self-testing through the coaching sessions

3. A self-review process of projects/tasks with a personal 'progress record' to complete and monitor

4. Free online resources to enhance the material in the book and provide model answers to some of the coaching sessions. Go to www.TYCoachbooks.com/Negotiation.

We will also offer a framework for observing and monitoring negotiation meetings led by colleagues and others who might have allowed you to act as an observer or witness. Coaching is a two-way process and you are encouraged to share the ideas in this book with others who are less experienced in achieving win/win results. Good luck with all your efforts as you work through this course and, more importantly, as you use the ideas and skills you have learned in your future negotiation projects!

Peter Fleming, MA, HRM, FCIM

1 WHO AM I?

 OUTCOMES FROM THIS CHAPTER

- Understand your attitude towards negotiating and how much of a priority you give it.
- Know your personal strengths and weaknesses that may affect your influence with others.
- Know to what extent you meet the expectations of others when expectations are constantly changing.
- Understand the climate affecting your market, environment, business culture and opportunities.
- Know the communication styles in common use.
- Understand how to use the coaching process to enhance your standing and current skills.

The amount we actually use our negotiation skills depends very much on:

- our personality (and that of the people around us)
- the environment (and culture) in which we were brought up and now live
- the expectations of our contacts (our family and friends as well as our boss and colleagues)
- the needs or objectives of our jobs or occupation, as set by our organization or business.

However, negotiating is one of those skills that is now expected to be in the skillset of all managers – and not just those with direct responsibility for sales and marketing, procurement or labour relations. It has become vital to master these skills in many fields of work and we also need these skills in our personal life. Working through this practical coaching book will enhance and develop your negotiating skills so that you will be more successful, not just at work, but in all areas of your life.

COACH'S TIP

Your reputation depends on your negotiating skills

Your credibility is at stake every time you negotiate on behalf of your organization, department or team and this means that your reputation is 'on the line' with every deal concluded.

COACHING SESSION 1

Icebreaker

Ask yourself whether you have ever experienced any of the following 'failures' in agreements that you were party to. Tick the boxes that apply to you and answer the question below it.

1. Lack of commitment from one of the parties? ☐

   How did this show itself?

   _____

   _____

2. A 'win/lose' culture applied in the meeting? ☐

   What behaviours were evident that led you to this conclusion?

   _____

   _____

3. Lack of detail in the agreement? ☐

   What was missing? And what were the consequences?

   _____

   _____

4. Insufficient power to implement the deal? ☐

   Was that acknowledged at the meeting? If not, why not?

   _____

   _____

What lessons were learned?

_____

_____

5. Fixed mindset applied by one (or even both) sides? ☐

   What effect did this have on the process?

   _____

   _____

6. Weak arguments used? ☐

   Were they identified and dealt with at the time? If not, why not?

   _____

   _____

7. Loss of control over minor issues? ☐

   How did this affect the use of time and level of achievement?

   _____

   _____

8. Ignoring influence of time and place? ☐

   What would have made a difference? How?

   _____

   _____

9. Giving up in the face of deadlock? ☐

   How did deadlock occur? How could it have been avoided?

   _____

   _____

10. Ignorance of the 'final authority'? ☐

    How could this have happened/been avoided?

    _____

    _____

11. Ignorance of how to use power? ☐

    Whose research/preparation/briefing was insufficient?

    _____

    _____

12. Ignorance of how/when to close? ☐

    What might the costs have been – or, more importantly, the lost opportunities?

    _____

    _____

If you found yourself checking some (or even all) of the above items, this book is definitely for you! If not, then you have been exceptionally fortunate in your business life. But has your domestic world been as easy? If you would prefer not to have to negotiate – with anyone or on anything – think again! The 'genie' has escaped from the bottle and needs confront us every day. This does not mean that you *have* to respond but you may be able to make significant improvements in arrangements you make, not only in business but in your private life as well.

COACHING SESSION 2

Setting goals

Set yourself some goals that you hope to achieve from the time you invest in this coaching manual.

List here some actions you will take and by when you will achieve them, and state how you'll measure how you achieved them.

Action	Date	Measure of achievement
1		
2		
3		
4		
5		

You might be thinking already that your life is one whole negotiation that never seems to stop. Dealing with tradespeople, with utility suppliers and the mechanics who service the car, making a doctor's appointment, seeking a pay rise from your employer, and trying to get your seven-year-old child to go to bed on time – all these things involve using the skills of negotiation. So let's start with a definition – a frame around which we can focus on the precise skills used by top negotiators.

⌂⌂ COACHING SESSION 3

Reflecting on your outlook on negotiation

Here is a first debating point:

1. Which of the following statements could be closest to your personal outlook?

    A 'Negotiation is an activity that we should engage in at all times, even when the opportunity for a "win" looks doubtful; if I don't try, I'll be reducing my chance of a gain.'

    B 'Negotiation is best avoided unless you have to do it, maybe as part of your job role; it can be time–consuming, embarrassing and deflating if and when you fail.'

2. Reflect on these statements and, if neither is really 'you', try to note down a brief description of someone you have met who does epitomize each of these statements:

    Person A _____

    _____

    _____

    Person B _____

    _____

    _____

3. How might you feel if you had to work opposite this person all the time? And what do you think might be the result?

    Person A _____

    _____

    _____

Person B _____

_____

_____

👥 COACHING SESSION 4

Where do you need negotiating skills?

Job roles and domestic situations vary considerably in terms of what kind of negotiation skills are required, but, in both spheres, you are likely to come across situations where you need excellent negotiating skills. The following situations typically require extensive negotiation skills:

Job roles

- Sales and marketing
- Purchasing and buying
- Senior management (especially brokering and managing change)
- Team management (especially when workload balance is involved)
- Representing colleagues (arbitration, discipline, employment conditions)

Domestic situations

- Maintaining family relationships through periods of pressure
- Relationship breakdown
- Living through building work at home
- Replacing the family car
- Moving house

Are you involved in any of these activities? If not, are you likely to be in the future? Describe possible future demands here:

_____

_____

_____

_____

_____

Before we address these current and future needs, we should also provide a similar opportunity for experienced negotiators.

QQ COACHING SESSION 5

How much negotiating do you do?

1. What proportion of your work time do you currently spend in planning, conducting and/or reviewing negotiations?

   Tick the appropriate box.

0–20%	21–40%	41–60%	61–80%	81–100%
☐	☐	☐	☐	☐

   Now put a cross against the category that you think will apply in six months' time. Does this indicate a likely increase or decrease?

2. What proportion of your time do you spend in planning, conducting and/or reviewing negotiations at home?

   Tick the appropriate box.

0–20%	21–40%	41–60%	61–80%	81–100%
☐	☐	☐	☐	☐

   Now put a cross against the category that you think will apply in six months' time. Does this indicate a likely increase or decrease?

3. Major changes suggest that your negotiation skills may also need to change. Note down here what changes you predict.

   At work:

   _____

   _____

   _____

   _____

   At home:

   _____

   _____

   _____

   _____

   _____

COACH'S TIP

Grow your skills

If you predict a major change in your work or home life, this suggests that your negotiation skills may need to grow, too. As you work through this book, use the action plan in the appendix to make notes about what you need to do.

You may have found that you use different levels of negotiating skills for the two different spheres. People with high negotiation profiles at work often seek to maintain a lower profile in their domestic or social roles. However, life is not always so easily managed: it may be fine to maintain a low profile in negotiations most of the time, but when a crisis arrives with frantic demands in the 'opposite' zone to your usual one, it can cause a high level of stress, which is potentially bad for your health. These thoughts may generate your motivation to revisit your work–life balance and make a commitment to work towards changing – with the aim to achieve better results through less stressful efforts.

COACHING SESSION 6

Self-assessment: managing stress

Negotiating demands a level of self-awareness of what you find stressful. Ask yourself the following questions:

1. Is much of my stress self-generated? ☐
2. Do I really have to question every action around me? ☐
3. Do arrangements at work/home frustrate me? ☐

If you ticked yes to one or more of these questions, how could you build a realistic plan for negotiating your way towards significant improvement?

_____

_____

_____

_____

_____

Add some notes to your action plan now.

ΩΩ COACHING SESSION 7

Setting personal objectives

Even if you have been negotiating for some time, you will benefit from setting some goals for yourself as you work through this manual. Use these questions as a guide.

1. What improvements would you like to make in your recent/current negotiations?

At work?

_____

_____

_____

In your social/domestic life?

_____

_____

_____

2. Who else is involved in these events and processes?

_____

_____

_____

3. What measurable improvements would you like to achieve in the future?

_____

_____

_____

_____

4. What additional support would be helpful? Who could provide it?

_____

_____

_____

_____

COACH'S TIP

Set your goals

Setting goals for your own development is vital if you are to avoid being 'trapped in a rut'. It is even more important if you are hoping to widen your experience and take on a bigger role with more responsibility.

WHY NEGOTIATE?

Negotiation takes considerable time and effort, so why do it, when there may be simpler, quicker alternatives? For example, you may instead choose to:

- impose a solution

- consult

- sell the idea.

Imposing a solution is quick but it involves the use of power. Results can include lack of motivation, conflict and lack of commitment to the imposed decision. Consulting is a frequently used alternative to negotiating and is rather less stressful, especially when the parties have a common interest in solving the problem, are prepared to discuss it openly and can invest in the time needed. Selling the idea is also a common method, which will succeed provided that the other party is 'conclusively sold' on the short- and long-term effects.

COACHING SESSION 8

Using alternative methods

If you used any of the alternative methods described above, what were the results? Would you use that method again and, if so, in what circumstances?

1. Imposing a solution

If you used this method, what were the results?

_____

_____

_____

_____

In what circumstances would you use that method again?

_____

_____

_____

2. **Consulting**

If you used this method, what were the results?

_____

_____

_____

In what circumstances would you use that method again?

_____

_____

_____

3. **Selling the idea**

If you used this method, what were the results?

_____

_____

_____

In what circumstances would you use that method again?

_____

_____

_____

There are other alternatives to negotiating that are also commonly used. They are:

- **acceptance**, when the other party accepts a proposal at first hearing – maybe through a power imbalance, fear of breaking the relationship, lethargy or viewing the deal as acceptable
- **mediation**, when a neutral third party consults with the parties – acting as a communications channel and proposing solutions reflecting the discussions
- **arbitration,** where a third party is appointed by the two main parties to make a decision binding on them all (a more extreme action would be recourse to law)
- **alternative dispute resolution**, when a third party consults and discusses solutions with both parties (separately and then together) and facilitates agreement without recourse to law. (This is especially valuable in cases of serious and costly disputes.)

COACHING SESSION 9

Other alternatives

1. Which of the other alternatives described above have you experienced?

_____

_____

_____

2. Were the outcomes satisfactory? If so, why, and if not, why not?

_____

_____

_____

3. How was the agreement implemented? Was it implemented in full?

_____

_____

_____

All the above tactics are perfectly acceptable – in the right circumstances. However, negotiating can bring unexpected consequences as well. For example, if you decide to negotiate where, previously, you imposed a solution, using the telling and directing management style, you should not be too surprised if your 'opponent' always wants to negotiate in the future. (Could this have occurred after that first time you allowed some flexibility for your child's normal bedtime?)

QQ COACHING SESSION 10

Self-assessment: your relationships

A review of your personal characteristics will help you assess your outlook on people and situations.

Consider the following ten characteristics that can determine the quality of your relationships with others. Shade in up to three numbers for each characteristic that you would normally expect to use in relations with others at work (and especially in a negotiation).

A. Understanding and awareness of others								
Unaware	1	2	3	4	5	6	7	Aware
B. Willingness to confront people and issues								
Unwilling	1	2	3	4	5	6	7	Willing
C. Control of relationships								
Always want to lead	1	2	3	4	5	6	7	Happy for others to lead
D. Flexibility								
Unwilling to change	1	2	3	4	5	6	7	Very willing to change
E. Tolerance of uncertainty								
Low	1	2	3	4	5	6	7	High
F. Self-confidence								
Low	1	2	3	4	5	6	7	High
G. Attitude to conflict								
Avoid conflict	1	2	3	4	5	6	7	Promote confrontation
H. Openness about feelings								
Reluctant	1	2	3	4	5	6	7	Open
I. How others see me								
Know how others see me	1	2	3	4	5	6	7	Don't know how others see me
J. Ability to listen								
Good listener	1	2	3	4	5	6	7	Poor listener

Now mark on the chart with a small cross the ratings you would apply to just one person with whom you negotiate regularly. Then consider what adjustments you might consider making for the relationship to achieve top results.

There is no one perfect score for all these ratings – and successful negotiators recognize the value of flexibility in style.

ONLINE RESOURCE

Model answers

The wise solution is to work with 'bands' of acceptability, as shown in the model answer for Coaching session 10 included in the online resources for this book. Compare your results with this and add any changes you feel you should make to your action plan. Go to:

www.TYCoachbooks.com/Negotiation

A REVIEW OF NEGOTIATING STYLES

For some less-than-confident negotiators, here is a short 'catch-up' of some key aspects of negotiating – most of which will reappear in subsequent chapters.

COACHING SESSION 11

Negotiating styles

How have you negotiated in the past, or seen negotiation in action? Tick the boxes against the descriptions that match your past experiences.

The application of power ☐

Adversarial bargaining ☐

Logical persuasion ☐

An exploration of mutually advantageous concessions ☐

A search for compromise ☐

Creative problem solving ☐

An exercise in attitude changing ☐

You could be forgiven for bringing to mind past experiences that have included all of the above – and also 'opponents' whose style has become 'stuck' in, maybe, a not very constructive approach. What I hope will be becoming clear is that there is unlikely to be just *one* preferred way of working which will be successful 100 per cent of the time, or which will be effective with every opponent.

There is one other dimensional aspect of negotiation style, the spectrum ranging from:

(more) **COMPETITIVE** ←————— to —————→ (more) **CO-OPERATIVE**

Competitive negotiators may:

- dominate their opponent
- open with tough demands
- have low interest in opponents' needs
- have preconceived solutions
- use power to gain compliance
- use statements rather than questions
- be disinterested in opponent's needs
- seek win/lose outcome (or lose/lose).

The attitude of each party towards the other can lie anywhere along this continuum, and may change in either direction (perhaps several times) as a relationship evolves over time.

You will no doubt have experienced both co-operative and competitive styles in your working life. Which has been most successful in your experience, and in what circumstances? For example, a negotiation between two organizations (which are going to depend on each other for the success of a deal) is more likely to gain from a collaborative relationship. A deal that is needed because of an emerging crisis may depend on speed and the expertise of the supplying party, which could be a reason for a less collaborative tone.

This is really about management style – the extent to which the negotiator is prepared to give up authority or power over a deal to accommodate their opponent's needs or desires. If the circumstances are serious (life or death), then it is probable that both negotiators will want to argue their case quite strongly; the issues being discussed will determine the methods adopted. However, some habitually competitive negotiators may want to use their strengths in the same way – leaving their opponents little alternative but to seek another supplier/ customer/staff representative/adviser. Result: lose/lose!

COACH'S TIP

Choose the right negotiating style

No one negotiating style is necessarily always the 'correct' one; it should be selected to meet most closely the specific requirements of each negotiating situation. Your style choice may well have an effect on the negotiation – in both the short and long term – and it should be carefully considered *before* formal discussion commences, so that you can assess the possible consequences.

The next coaching session may help you identify gaps in your skillset – which should become goals for self-improvement. To make things clearer, they are divided into two areas: first tactics and then style and behaviour. Which of these approaches have you experienced or used most frequently?

COACHING SESSION 12

Self-assessment: your preferred style

1. Read the following list of negotiation tactics. Tick the boxes for those tactics you are most comfortable using. Mark with crosses those you would not choose to use.

   Using open questions: Who? What? Why? How? Where? ☐

   Setting objectives ☐

   Making concessions ☐

   Using (or hinting at) threats/promises ☐

   Deliberate non-verbal communication (e.g. gestures) ☐

   Exposing emotion (e.g. uncontrolled) ☐

   Deliberately maintaining silence ☐

   Concentrated listening ☐

   Partnering with additional people (e.g. colleagues) ☐

   Building close relationships (e.g. reinforced socially) ☐

   Add notes on the crossed tactics (x) you identified to your personal action plan.

2. Now tick the boxes below that correspond to the frequency with which you adopt the following styles and behaviours at the negotiating table:

	Often	Rarely	Sometimes
Sell your ideas	☐	☐	☐
Ask questions	☐	☐	☐
Be positive, not negative	☐	☐	☐
Keep objectives in mind	☐	☐	☐
Keep control	☐	☐	☐
Make concessions, one at a time	☐	☐	☐
Identify opponents' objectives	☐	☐	☐
Avoid being 'conditioned'	☐	☐	☐
Never use bluff or brinkmanship without considering the consequences	☐	☐	☐
Negotiate; do not argue	☐	☐	☐
Be clear and concise	☐	☐	☐
Be persistent	☐	☐	☐
Summarize and confirm	☐	☐	☐

Now make a commitment to introduce the preferred tactics and behaviours you listed that you believe could be helpful. Note them on your personal action plan.

! COACH'S TIP

Always implement the agreement

In addition to a track record of negotiating agreements, your record of implementation should be exemplary. In a sense, the best chance of full implementation arises when the negotiation is a 'win/win' experience and result. Anything less could risk either side looking hard for excuses for *not* fully implementing the agreement. Such a result could end in a 'lose/lose' outcome.

🗩🗩 COACHING SESSION 13

Reflection

Think about the results of the previous coaching session and how you can use this knowledge.

1. What is your greatest challenge in seeking to improve your negotiation skills?

   _____

   _____

2. How could you increase your exposure and gain more practice in a 'safe' environment?

   _____

   _____

3. Now that you have started to think more about 'who you are', how could you start to use your experiences to exploit your strengths and eradicate your weak areas?

   _____

   _____

THE SKILLED NEGOTIATOR

Negotiation is part of a particular type of human relationship characterized by specific behaviours/activities and usually enduring over a period of time. We can see now that, implicit in the success of a negotiator are the face-to-face behaviours, attitudes, tactics, techniques and strategies used during negotiation.

Research about skilled negotiators shows that success comes from:

- being rated as effective by *both* sides
- having a track record of significant success
- having a low incidence of implementation failure.

UNDERSTANDING YOUR 'MARKET'

Over the last few decades, negotiation has become a formalized and recognized skill across all business sectors, and beyond. The consequence is that there has been greater movement of people across all sectors – from industry to commerce and into non-industrial sectors. Few, if any, sectors now do not need support from highly skilled negotiators.

As a result, there is now considerable 'cross-fertilization' of skills across all sectors and occupations. Typically, in the past, we might have expected sharper, compulsive 'push' – or dictatorial – styles of negotiation to be the mark of lower-profit margin industries (such as food retailing) and lower-key, affiliative styles to be more evident in high-value sectors such as property and financial services. This means that there is much less certainty today about the chosen negotiating style of an opponent, which may be quite unpredictable because of their previous experience in a totally different sector.

COACHING SESSION 14

Identifying top negotiators

The following table lists ten different negotiating styles, some of which are more likely to bring better results than others – but which?

Decide in which of the following two categories the styles belong and tick the appropriate column:

    A – Behaviours and styles most likely to bring the best results
    B – Behaviours and styles most likely to bring average results.

Negotiating style	Characteristics	A	B
Safety first/ survivor	Wants to play it safe at all costs		
Controller	Wants to control everything, down to the smallest and least important detail		
Expert/teacher	Cannot resist telling their opponents all about their past experience and (successful) deals		
Extrovert	Is notable for talking much more than listening		
Completer/ finisher	Generally seeks the highest results from regular negotiations, with usually sound results		
Escapologist	Talks a good 'game' and may take risks		
Opportunist	May be motivated by timing: 'It's now or never', or 'We'll miss the boat if we have to go through the fine detail.'		
Innocent	Could be a genuine learner or an experienced person posing as naive.		
Politician	Needs to be 'politically correct', even when unconventional methods are required		
Pessimist	Looks on the negative side of things most of the time and resists showing excitement or enthusiasm		

Check your answers with the model answer given in the online resources for this chapter. Go to www.TYCoachbooks.com/Negotiation

COACH'S TIP

Be flexible

To be a successful negotiator, you need to be able to adapt your style (or at least adopt a more flexible style) to fit the variety of styles that may be used by the various opponents you may have to deal with.

The following fictional case study illustrates the skills described in this book, and is followed by some questions for you to consider. Each chapter follows the success (or otherwise) of the discussions – leading to a result on the last day.

CASE STUDY: THE FIRST MEETING

Background

The client: Builders' General Supplies (BuGS) provides building materials mainly for small independent building contractors in a major city, its surrounding towns and the county. The new Managing Director has been expanding the company over the last year and is investing heavily in a new sales force (both area representatives and newly trained counter sales assistants). His next step is a uniform recording system for progressing all sales records against targets. No common system exists across the branches and his analysis is that just a paper system would improve things 100 per cent (especially if it could be progressed into a computer system later on).

The supplier: Supreme Systems Ltd markets computer-based sales-recording systems for medium-sized companies currently using record cards (which are then processed electronically at a central data-processing centre). Recent developments have introduced hand-held terminals that will enable electronic transmission down a telephone line (provisionally known as 'point-of-order terminals' or POTs).

The meeting

Supreme's sales negotiator (Jan) arranges a meeting with Mac, (General Manager of BuGS' largest site) and takes along her laptop to demonstrate the system she wants to supply. At the end of the demo, they have the following exchange:

Jan: Have I convinced you that this system would speed up order processing 100 per cent?

Mac: It's certainly an interesting idea.

Jan: Most sales reps can't fault the level of detail recorded on those state-of-the-art manual cards as, once the customer has signed the order off, there could be a next-day delivery. Wouldn't your customers be impressed by that?

Mac: You'd be surprised – most want the stuff yesterday!

Jan: The start-up cost includes the basic training of all the reps – which, at your head office, will provide a great opportunity for celebrations and a social – bringing a great lift in morale. That's good, isn't it?

Mac: It's a long time since we had a jolly!

Jan: All you need is to sign up for a year's supply of the paper system to get started now and a letter of intent for the terminals (POTs). We can leave the installation account for the full computer system until later on. That'll save any possible complications – OK?

Mac: Sounds good to me – but we'll have to involve the new computer manager when he starts.

Jan: You'll be joining 45 per cent of the progressive part of the industry by introducing this breakthrough system and I'm sure you'll be pleased with it within days of its implementation. Shall we head off for some lunch now...?"

Mac: Best idea I've heard so far – where are you going to take me this time?

Confidential interview with the new Managing Director at BuGS

'Mac, the General Manager here, holds things together well. With a history in the sales field, customers still like the personal attention they get from him when they come here. However, I'm yet to be convinced that his skillset matches the wider range of duties now involved in the job.'

Confidential report from Supreme's Sales Manager

'The rep (Jan) is very active. Sales for the Record Card Department grow consistently but I'd like to see more conversions into the computer application – that's where the money and the future is!'

 COACH'S TIP

Remember the winning formula

Remember that the winning formula for top results is: 'A top-line strategy, matched with highly skilled negotiators, brings industry-leading results.'

COACHING SESSION 15

Analysing the case study: the first meeting

Read the case study above and answer the following questions:

1. What evidence did either character reveal of understanding or implementing a successful business strategy?

_____

_____

_____

_____

2. What action (if any) would you recommend each should take?

_____

_____

_____

_____

3. Review the meeting and decide whether each character fits into any of the ten profiles introduced earlier in this chapter. They are listed below, with space for you to nominate 'casting' roles. Not all these roles may have been evident at the meeting – and one person could have more than one profile.

Role	Your nomination
1 Safety first/survivor	
2 Controller	
3 Expert/teacher	
4 Extrovert	
5 Completer/finisher	
6 Escapologist	
7 Opportunist	
8 Innocent	
9 Politician	
10 Pessimist	

Now check your answers with the analysis and review in the online resource for this chapter. Go to www.TYCoachbooks.com/Negotiation

ONLINE RESOURCE

Take a test

Now that you have an overview of some key issues that can affect your success as a negotiator, take this online negotiation test which will help you identify your current profile: go to www.psychologytoday.tests, select TESTS and search for 'Negotiating Skills Test', which will provide you with a fast evaluation using a multi-choice questionnaire – without any longer-term commitment. Add the result and any recommendation to your personal action plan.

PREPARING TO NEGOTIATE

Before going into any negotiation, ask yourself the following questions:

1. Have we negotiated on these issue(s) before?

2. Are there any precedents? If not, why make one now?

3. Are our opponents seeking to renegotiate an existing agreement? If so, why?

4. Is the purpose of a renegotiation to tighten up the working of an existing agreement?

5. Is there a timescale for settlement of the negotiation?

6. Does this provide a framework for negotiation meetings?

7. Is there a commitment to it on both sides?

8. Have we implemented it without exception?

PROD-ProSC: A MAP FOR NEGOTIATION

The acronym PROD-ProSC describes the essential steps in a negotiation and is a useful shorthand way of memorizing a sequential approach to the whole process. It stands for:

1. **Prepare**

2. **Research**

3. **Open**

4. **Discuss and debate**

5. **Propose**

6. **Summarize**

7. **Close**

This step-by-step approach to negotiation makes sure that you go through a logical process that will be less likely to cause trouble later on than a more random approach. Short cuts may be tempting, but can also be a cause for regret. This does not mean that all meetings must follow this pattern, but having a map is a useful way of thinking about the steps you need to take to complete the process without mistakes or exceptions. The stages are shown in the following table. The table is repeated in each chapter, with the step(s) covered in that chapter highlighted in bold.

STAGE	ISSUES
P = Prepare a) People b) Place	 What do I know about the culture and style of representatives of this business/organization? How affected am I likely to be by the personal comfort factors – e.g. distractions, noise and interruptions, seating/layout?
R = Research	What is our opponents' position?
0 = Open	How should I open the meeting? What ice-breaking topics might be used? Are there any probing questions I could ask? How could we establish some common ground?
D = Discuss and debate	What style of conversation should I adopt?
Pro = Propose Conflict management	How will I resist the temptation to move too quickly/slowly? What if we disagree in a major way?
S = Summarize	How good am I at using summaries in meetings?
C = Close	What methods of closing can I use most effectively?

ONLINE RESOURCES

Additional techniques and model answers

There are online resources to help you gain greater depth of understanding of this first chapter, with some additional techniques and guides to the coaching sessions. They include:

- advice on developing the right attitude to negotiating
- a personal skills development plan, which you can use to assess your negotiating skills in comparison with the skills of your opponents
- model answers to Coaching session 10
- model answers to Coaching session 14
- an analysis and a review of the case study.

Go to:

www.TYCoachbooks.com/Negotiation

NEXT STEPS

This first chapter has tested your understanding of the negotiating process and offered some fundamental ideas about what it involves. However, those concepts seek to challenge your ability both to select the concepts which best fit your environment and also to build an operating position that will bring best results – without making your opponents feel that they have 'lost ground'.

The next chapter continues that trend by re-emphasizing the importance of preparation and research in preparing a powerful negotiating plan.

TAKEAWAYS

What are *your* greatest needs in preparing for negotiation meetings?

_____

_____

_____

_____

_____

How much time can you invest in such preparation at work?

_____

_____

_____

_____

_____

How much time can you invest in such preparation at home?

_____

_____

_____

_____

_____

How would you like that balance to change, while still achieving the best results?

_____

_____

_____

_____

_____

What personal strengths have you identified in reflecting on this chapter?

_____

_____

_____

_____

What weaknesses have you now identified?

_____

_____

_____

_____

What steps will you take in studying this book?

_____

_____

_____

_____

What steps will you take in applying the lessons of this chapter to your job?

_____

_____

_____

_____

Which styles of negotiation are you most comfortable using?

_____

_____

_____

_____

_____

2 PREPARATION AND RESEARCH

✔ OUTCOMES FROM THIS CHAPTER

- Grasp the advantage of careful research contributing to a structured negotiating plan.
- Understand the motives behind a proposed deal and the explicit and implicit needs arising.
- Assess short- and longer-term goals (organizational and for the individual).
- Analyse authority: how decisions are made and by whom, and who will sign them off.
- Assess your readiness to negotiate before the meeting.

Some people seem to be born negotiators and it is in their nature to negotiate over everything. The rest of us do it from time to time and, depending upon the importance of the topic and situation, we know that the difference between reaching a satisfactory result and a 'whitewash' will be the research and preparation that we have completed beforehand. This chapter shows you how to develop a disciplined approach to preparation – and some key points that can make the difference between 'winning' and 'losing'.

Since a negotiation is really an exercise in moving your 'opponent' towards a pre-planned position – that is, agreeing to a deal that meets all your objectives – there is much to be said for the ability to have an easy, stress-free conversation with your opposite number in a business meeting. Of course, the best deals are those that satisfy *both* parties' needs – a real win/win.

COACHING SESSION 16

Reviewing the case study

A neutral observer would have several criticisms of the interactions in the case study in Chapter 1. Review the phrasing of the interactions from the case study (set out below) and consider what additional information *might* have been revealed. For example, the first question asked is a closed one, which will not achieve as much as an open question.

For each exchange, note down what you think it will achieve and what different phraseology might be better, and why.

1. **Jan:** Have I convinced you that this system would speed up order processing 100 per cent?

_____

_____

_____

_____

_____

_____

2. **Mac:** It's certainly an interesting idea.

_____

_____

_____

_____

_____

_____

3. **Jan:** Most sales reps can't fault the level of detail recorded on those state-of-the-art manual cards as, once the customer has signed the order off, there could be a next-day delivery. Wouldn't your customers be impressed by that?

_____

_____

_____

_____

_____

_____

4. **Mac:** You'd be surprised – most want the stuff yesterday!

_____

_____

_____

_____

_____

_____

5. **Jan:** The start-up cost includes the basic training of all the reps – which, at your head office, will provide a great opportunity for celebrations and a social – bringing a great lift in morale. That's good, isn't it?

_____

_____

_____

_____

_____

_____

6. **Mac:** It's a long time since we had a jolly!

_____

_____

_____

_____

_____

7. **Jan:** All you need is to sign up for a year's supply of the paper system to get started now and a letter of intent for the terminals (POTs). We can leave the installation account for the full computer system until later on. That'll save any possible complications – OK?

_____

8. **Mac:** Sounds good to me – but we'll have to involve the new computer manager when he starts.

9. **Jan:** You'll be joining 45 per cent of the progressive part of the industry by introducing this breakthrough system and I'm sure you'll be pleased with it within days of its implementation. Shall we head off for some lunch now?

10. **Mac:** Best idea I've heard so far – where are you going to take me this time?

Compare your answers with the commentary in the online resources for this chapter.
Go to www.TYCoachbooks.com/Negotiation

TEN COMMON MISTAKES

To help you improve your skills, here is a reminder of ten things to avoid during a negotiation. Which of us can say that we really have never done any of these things?

1. Fixed mindset
2. Ignorance of final authority
3. Ignorance of how to use power
4. Opening with general or final goals
5. Not using substantial arguments
6. Losing control over unimportant factors
7. Making the first offer
8. Ignoring time and place
9. Giving up in the face of deadlock
10. Not knowing when to close

THINKING ABOUT OPPONENTS: THE ARCH-NEGOTIATORS

Arch-negotiators are exceptional people whose nature is to negotiate over practically everything. In both business (and personal) situations, negotiations can be very expensive and time-consuming – not just during the negotiation but also before it and afterwards, especially if mistakes are made. For this reason, habitual negotiators sharpen their skills – but they do not always discriminate between the different issues or situations in which they negotiate (and they may also take on causes that consume more time than can really be beneficial against the results to be achieved).

The amount of time people spend using their negotiation skills often depends on:

■ the culture and environment in which they were brought up and now live (in some countries it is the norm for everyone to negotiate over practically everything)

■ their personality (and that of those around them)

■ the expectations of their contacts (e.g. family and friends)

■ needs or objectives arising from the job/occupation/career (imposed by the organization or business).

A key distinguishing feature between highly skilled negotiators and the rest lies in the amount of research and preparation they do, especially for their most important and valuable projects (which are also those most likely to involve formal meetings). **Thorough research and preparation are vital components of a successful outcome.**

COACHING SESSION 17

Formal versus informal negotiation

Consider the following factors in preparing for both a formal and an informal negotiation. Complete the following table, thinking about the advantages you would identify for a new negotiator who might be concerned to avoid any potential risks when dealing with a new contact and/or organization.

Factors to consider	Advantages of formal negotiation (e.g. there may be past records of meetings with these people, enabling some briefing)	Advantages of informal negotiation (e.g. opponents may be off their guard)
1. People (e.g. backup/support)		
2. Places (e.g. quiet/confidentiality)		
3. Things (e.g. samples/systems)		
4. Customs (e.g. methods/trust-building)		
5. Practice (e.g. trust arising from past meetings)		
6. Influence (e.g. status and confidence)		
7. Negotiation style (e.g. introverted vs extrovert)		
8. Organizational support (e.g. information systems)		
9. Availability of information (e.g. backup/accessibility)		

 COACH'S TIP

Beware the risks of informal meetings

Probably the biggest risk of informal meetings is that one or both of the participants fails to make sufficient preparations because they think that since it is an informal meeting they can therefore 'wing it'. This is a big mistake – and best avoided because with this attitude you can miss valuable experiences, attitudes and information, which could be harvested at little or no cost.

THE IMPORTANCE OF RESEARCH

When you are preparing to work with a new organization (supplier *or* client), you may not have much first-hand experience or data to use in the above preparation plan. This does not make the process irrelevant, but you may have to fill the gaps with additional research and maybe a little educated guesswork. Arch-negotiators may try to tempt you to adopt short cuts – but be aware that the results could benefit them rather more than you.

Even if you are an experienced negotiator, a negotiating plan (and fundamental data already collected) will still provide a useful brief to test out assumptions at the first negotiating meeting. This is a good opportunity to compare your opponent's answers to key questions alongside the preparation/predictions made from your own research. Any serious distortions or surprises in the verbal answers that appear to conflict with the basic research that has been gathered may indicate the need for closer questioning (and more detailed research in terms of other sources). None of this is about mistrusting other negotiators – but only checking the accuracy of what they tell you.

 COACH'S TIP

Look out for misleading information

One exaggeration or untruth can so easily lead to a whole string of them. Misleading information of any kind from your opponent (supplier or client) may contra-indicate any future dealings or contracts with them.

Many negotiators prefer to use a pre-prepared framework for this kind of research, so that important loose ends are not overlooked in favour of some instinct that all is well. If the new contact deliberately denies the evidence of your research, this will provide you with a contra-indication for future dealings. Here is a typical format for this type of research used by top negotiators:

	Our issue?	Their issue?
Motives	Fill a gap in stock range planned for summer sale	Clear old stock and enable cash to be reinvested
Ultimate goal	100% return on cost	Maximum 15% reduction (e.g. quantities/values) on old selling price
Timing	Deliver in 8 weeks + pay in 12 weeks	Best price for immediate payment and collection by client
Conditions	Extend suppliers' 'standard' guarantees to include refund	As seen only at lowest price

⌬⌬ COACHING SESSION 18

Your preparation framework

Use the format shown above to complete your own table for a current or forthcoming project. It will show you the gaps in your knowledge that you will need to research. Record these in your personal action plan.

	Our issue?	Their issue?
Motives		
Ultimate goal		
Timing		
Conditions		

BUILDING RELATIONSHIPS

Unless your negotiations involve players who have met before and are used to negotiating together, you will need to build new relationships with the people you are negotiating with. A thoroughly researched approach to a first meeting will pay dividends time and time again. This means finding out who your clients are, in order to:

- save time in preparing proposals that are unlikely to match their needs
- build common ground
- demonstrate willingness to develop a mutual trading strategy (best done when there is clear understanding and trust between the parties).

To gain fullest understanding, information may be assembled under three simple headings:

- Past
- Present
- Future.

The case study from Chapter 1 continues below. It shows how one of the parties could use these three headings to draw together facts and narratives gained from informal discussions with local customers and tradespeople.

CASE STUDY: BuGS (THE CLIENT)

Past

The original builders' supplies business was founded in the 1930s by Thomas Buggs, who foresaw opportunities in his region for house building. He astutely identified the need for a regional merchant structure for the supply of building materials – backed with careful credit terms and management to maximize cash flow and minimize bad debts. His extrovert personality ensured his popularity with customers, who welcomed his accessibility and the 'special deals' that he always maintained for his regulars.

During and after the Second World War, the business survived better than most, through periods of tight credit squeezes and strict controls on materials. Mr Buggs gradually delegated more responsibility to his two sons – who diversified the business into 'light-side' materials: ironmongery and plumbing supplies. Growth was steady but the differing personalities and competitiveness of the two sons threatened to drive older/more traditional customers away, causing something of a family rift.

Present

Trading difficulties experienced by competing merchants provided opportunities for expansion across the region and the business went public in the 1990s. This brought major change – in staff and management structure – and the appointment of a new board, bringing in badly needed management experience and skills. Through all these changes, the founding family has been at great pains to try to maintain the atmosphere of a family business – with customers maintaining informal contact with senior management.

Future

Formal budgeting has been introduced down to branch levels. Clients have heard from sales reps that when new computer-based systems are introduced there is a 'probability of erratic deliveries and supplies' (and 'probably for a good six months afterwards'). The reps have said that the best way around this is 'to order early and optimistically'! A realistic analysis seems to be that the company is likely to go through a period of 'growing pains'.

How does information about a company affect outcomes? A potential supplier (or major client) who is aware of certain stories about an opponent could be tempted to exploit any fears and difficulties that might arise. But who knows what will really happen? A client business will be anxious to prove the pessimists wrong – and, if it is a public company, any bad news could have a dramatic effect upon the value of the business (as in its share price). So there is much to gain – and, potentially, to lose.

COACHING SESSION 19

Planning a new project

While negotiation can be an enjoyable challenge, it can also be very time-consuming with all the hidden work involved. You might want to ask yourself the following questions before rushing into a new project:

1. Have we negotiated on this issue before? ☐

2. Are there any precedents? ☐

3. Are our opponents seeking to renegotiate an existing agreement? ☐

4. If so, do we know why? ☐

5. Is the purpose to tighten up the working of an existing agreement? ☐

6. If so, has there been a unilateral attempt to impose the full agreement against convention? ☐

7. Do we have a timescale for settlement of the negotiation? ☐

8. Does this provide a framework for negotiation meetings? ☐

9. Is there a commitment to this on both sides? ☐

10. Have *we* honoured the timing? ☐

If you ticked yes to most of these questions, going forward with your negotiation plan is likely to repay the effort involved. If you answered no to most of them, the remaining coaching sessions in this chapter will help you with your next project, if not the current one.

COACH'S TIP

Make yourself credible

Credibility of experience is everything, even if the actual system/service you are selling might be less than perfect for your client's needs. For example, it might be:

- too expensive
- unavailable when the need is greatest
- incompatible with the existing (computer) system.

Clients have been known to introduce systems that are not perfect, simply because they have access to advice from a credible resource.

You'll be able to predict a variety of outcomes – but the critical issue is how additional knowledge about a client could help a tendering company pitch the potential supply of sales administration materials to match that client's needs. Past experience would enable the sales consultant to predict this selling point – but not the current urgency nor the opportunity to talk credibly about past clients who have been through this change successfully (as a result of the consultant's support).

COACHING SESSION 20

Evaluating impacts on sales motives

Answer these questions to evaluate sales motives and their effects.

1. What factors would you use to sell-in your supplying company services to ensure an advantageous negotiation with this client?

2. What kind of 'story/experience' about your organization could potentially make a client reluctant to deal with you?

3. As the client, how would you assess that the sales consultant had first-hand experience of all the factors they describe (as opposed to learning them second-hand or from a book)?

GATHERING DATA TO FILL GAPS

Gathering data enables gaps or guesses to be properly identified and addressed –
before the meeting. However, some items may be confidential and can be discovered
only with carefully placed questions during the negotiation itself.

An obvious constraint of this approach is that items described or verbal promises
made in meetings may turn out to be completely false or plainly misleading. This
important area may be dependent upon trust – unless independent research has
produced reassuring evidence. Key elements and questions that have a bearing
on the success (or otherwise) of the planned deal also need to be prepared in
advance of the meeting itself.

ΩΩ COACHING SESSION 21

Early stages checklist

The following checklist makes a useful memory jogger for a meeting. Fill in the points you
need to remember. Check the following points and add your notes to your action plan in the
appendix.

Questions and issues	Answers
P = Prepare	
a) People?	
Who am I meeting?	
What authority do they have?	
Who else is likely to be present?	
What do we know about the culture and style of this organization/business and, particularly, the people who run it?	
ITEMS NEEDED	
b) Documentation?	

c) Samples?	
d) Notes on client?	
e) Illustrations of service to others?	

 ONLINE RESOURCE

Early stages checklist

Find a copy of this checklist in the online resources for this chapter. Print it out and use as a prompt when preparing for future meetings. Go to:

www.TYCoachbooks.com/Negotiation

Planning checklist

Find a copy of this planning sheet in the online resources. Print it off every time you need to prepare for a meeting and take it to the meeting with you..

Factor	Points I must ask about or listen for
1 Opening, interest and needs How should I open the meeting? How interested is the other party in the meeting? What needs might exist?	

2 Authority Who am I meeting? What is the history/track record of the relationship? How much authority does he/she have?	
3 Power and influence What is their 'power' over us and/or our competitors? What is our power? How can we exploit our strength for mutual benefit?	
4 Commitment How interested is he/she in the issue to be resolved? How badly do they need an agreement? Do we want agreement today?	
5 Competition/exclusivity How might market forces effect the negotiation? What leverage might be used?	
6 Innovation and promotion How novel is the service/product? What concessions are we likely to have to make to ensure the success of the deal? Who will contribute what to help?	

COACHING SESSION 22

Understanding the client

For successful negotiation, you need to understand your client's motives, needs, goals and authority levels. This knowledge will help you put yourself into their shoes and build rapport.

Make short notes in the table below about your client knowledge, rating your certainty of each factor on the scale A–D as follows:

- A = **positive evidence** of this
- B = **educated guess** based on experience elsewhere
- C = **need to uncover evidence** on this in the next meeting
- D = **item needing sensitive questioning** in this and other meetings.

The client	What I know	Rating A–D
Their motives		
Their needs		
Their short-term goals		
Their longer-term goals		

CASE STUDY: THE PROJECT MEETING

Several weeks after the last meeting, the new IT Manager has joined the company and another project meeting takes place, with the following people present:

For BuGS (the client)

- Andy: Finance Director (Chair)
- Noel: IT Manager (new appointment)
- Mac: General Manager, Site No.1

For Supreme Systems (the supplier)

- Jan: Sales Manager

- Billy: Technical Manager

1. Andy: Firstly, can I welcome you both to BuGS' Head Office? My name is Andy and I'm the Corporate Finance Director for this independent business. My colleagues are Mac, who I think you have met – General Manager of this site here – and our most recent appointment, Noel, who has joined us as our new IT Manager.

2. Billy: Wow! That's quick – Have you got an IT strategy?

3. Andy   (*defensively*) Well, we haven't, yet – but it's business in hand! We haven't met before, have we?

4. Jan: No, sorry about that – I was about to introduce us – I am Sales Manager for Supreme and responsible for all development of service contracts with our clients – and Billy here is our Technical Manager, who…

5. Billy: Yeah, I've been working with Mac there and his team in designing a 'cardex'-type system which would be an ideal starting point for an eventual Supreme computer sales system. You know this is very widely used in Distribution and we pride ourselves that we have over ten years' successful experience in helping independent businesses just like yours. Only the other day…

6. Andy: Yes, I've heard all about that from Mac – but things have changed now; we are not going to go with a document system – Mac and I have been working on a paper for our Board that will set out a new strategy. Do you want to say something about that, Mac?

7. Mac: Sure! Jan and I have had several meetings in which we have thrown about various ideas and, rather than go through two system changes, we're now thinking it'll be easier if we go for a 'big bang' and migrate to a full point-of-sale system. That could be with Supreme or we could put it out to tender, maybe starting…

8. Billy: (*interrupting*) Oh dear, after all that work – I hope you'll remember that when we tender – we already have a lot of knowledge of the company and some of your salespeople are not going to like such a big changeover all in one go! And Supreme has a lot of credibility with your sort of staff – you know, 'hands-on, call a spade a shovel'. You need to keep 'em 'on-side' and *we* know how to do that.

9. Noel: I'm sure you do – but things have changed here – my last project with my last company was doing exactly as you have described – and we actually halved the installation time … it was very successful.

10. Billy: (*aside to Jan*) Huh! So successful that he's left there and come here on the strength of it – before the s**t hits the fan, I dare say!

11. Jan: (*hastily*) Well, whatever transpires, we'd like to think that, with our working knowledge of this traditional family business, our team could look after your needs – and tailor-make something that will see you through till your next store opening. When's that going to be, by the way?

12. Mac: Next –

13. Andy: Er, we haven't made that kind of announcement yet – there's still a lot of water to pass under the bridge – and we like to keep our competitors on their toes.

14. Billy: (*loud whisper*) Bet it's Birmingham!

15. Mac: There's some good pubs there – after our last trip – you remember, Billy, that fella who was trying to get in with us in that bar?

16. Noel: (*interrupting*) What I'd like to hear more about, Andy, is Supreme's capability to build interactive computer programs in-house – I assume you have that facility?

17. Billy: Do we? We founded the National Computer School of Little Brightwell! It makes millions for us every year! And we are pilot-testing point-of-order terminals, or POTs for short!

18. Jan: (*hastily*) We like to think that the school is one of our 'good deeds' – we'd use their staff for your staff training (as a loss leader, of course) if we won the contract. Can you tell us more about the system and hardware you are using so that we can prepare a proposal?

(*The meeting continues for another ten minutes in this vein until Mac has to leave to apologize to a customer whose vehicle has been blocked in by Billy and Jan's car. After some hasty goodbyes, the BuGS team sit down to review the brief meeting.*)

19. Andy: Well, what did we make of that lot? It's just as well the MD wasn't here! I think he'd have called security to see them off the premises! Am I being too hard?

20. Noel: No! There's certainly no 'polish' about Billy, is there? But, he's right about having the salespeople on his side. That could be useful.

21. Andy: Yes, but we haven't time for niceties – once the Board approves, we've got to get moving quickly. They'll want to see it all up and running within three months.

(*Meanwhile, Billy and Jan drive off with the intention of talking over the meeting in a café on the other side of town. They congratulate themselves on how well the relationship is developing, then…*)

22. Jan: By the way, how did you get on with that new terminal I lent you – it's the latest pilot model from Ouzi Computers and will probably be the model we'll eventually supply to BuGS when the contract comes in.

23. Billy: I think it's a great piece of kit – great packaging – and, despite the fact that the software isn't properly compatible yet, I've found a way of making it talk to my laptop and also download data.

24. Jan: I didn't ask you to do that! I had better have it back before you do any lasting damage!

25. Billy: Relax, boss, as if I would; you are great at giving us these insights into the new systems – it puts us ahead of sales teams in other parts of the country.

COACHING SESSION 23

Analysing the case study teams

Having read the transcript of the meeting above, write short notes about the supplier team and the host team, using the numbered entries as prompts.

1. What evidence is there of research and preparation for the meeting by either team?

   Host team

   _____

   Supplier team

   _____

2. What was their strategy and approach to the meeting?

   Host team

   _____

   Supplier team

   _____

3. Which approaches to influencing did they seemed be using?

   Host team

   _____

   Supplier team

   _____

4. What did they learn from the discussion?

   Host team

   _____

   Supplier team

   _____

5. What progress might they have made?

   Host team

   _____

Supplier team

_____

6. What advice would you offer to either side to make forward progress more likely?

Host team

_____

Supplier team

_____

COACHING SESSION 24

Analysing the roles

From the meeting we can visualize the characters and how they might be thinking in real life. Think about each person from the perspective of the following profiles. (Remember that not all these roles may have been evident at the meeting – and one person could have more than one role).

Role	Your nomination
1 Safety first/survivor	
2 Controller	
3 Expert/teacher	
4 Extrovert	
5 Completer/finisher	
6 Escapologist	
7 Opportunist	
8 Innocent/naïve person	
9 Politician	
10 Pessimist	

Now check your answers with the model answers in the online resources.

☺☺ COACHING SESSION 25

Applying the lessons

What steps will you now take to apply what you have learned so far to your own projects? Use the prompts below to write down the results of your research.

1. Motives behind a proposed deal

2. Explicit and implicit needs arising

3. Short- and longer-term goals (organizational and for the individual)

4. Analysis of authority (i.e. how decisions are made and by whom – and who will authorize them) so that you can assess the client's readiness *before* the negotiation meeting.

FINAL PREPARATIONS

Before rushing to your meeting, make sure that you have the answers to these final questions:

1. Have we established the 'going rates'?

2. What are the views of top analysts/commentators?

3. Do we have our market projections?

4. What access do we have to inside knowledge?

5. Are we prepared to move from the starting position?

6. Have we prepared a strategy for obtaining movement?

7. Could we link any issues?

8. Can we use hypothetical arguments (e.g. 'Supposing...?')

9. Have we prepared a strategy for using adjournments?

10. Could sanctions be applied as part of the bargaining process?

11. How do the parties view the need to bargain fairly?

12. At its worst, what would our 'best alternative to a negotiated settlement' (BATNeS) be?

Use your action plan

Make notes on all the above points in your action plan in the appendix.

 ONLINE RESOURCES

The case study

Now check the online resources for additional planning documents and routines and the next phase of the negotiation case study. Go to:

www.TYCoachbooks.com/Negotiation

THE PROD-ProSC MAP

The acronym PROD-ProSC describes the process of a negotiation. This does not mean that all meetings must follow this pattern but it is a useful way of thinking about the steps you need to take to complete the process without mistakes or exceptions. The stages are shown in the table below. Your current position on the map is highlighted in bold.

Stage	Issues
P = Prepare a) **People** b) **Place**	**What do I know about the culture and style of representatives of this business/organization?** **How affected am I likely to be by the personal comfort factors – e.g. distractions, noise and interruptions, seating/layout?**
R = Research	What is our opponents' position? What are their motives, needs and goals? Who are the key authorizing players?
0 = Open	How should I open the meeting? What ice-breaking topics might be used? Are there any probing questions I could ask? How could we establish some common ground?
D = Discuss and debate	What style of conversation should I adopt?
Pro = Propose	How will I resist the temptation to move too quickly/slowly?
(Conflict management)	What if we disagree in a major way?
S = Summarize	How good am I at using summaries in meetings?
C = Close	What methods of closing can I use most effectively?

Once you have explored your current stage, note in your action plan any areas that might need more attention.

→ NEXT STEPS

Now that you have done your preparation and assessed what you need to do to be ready to negotiate, it is time to research and plan your objectives. This means identifying the motives behind a proposed deal and the goals of both you and the other party, as well as knowing how decisions are made. Using this knowledge, you will be able to create a structured negotiation plan.

👍 **TAKEAWAYS**

How will your research contribute to a structured negotiating plan?

_____

_____

_____

_____

_____

_____

_____

_____

_____

How will you discover the needs and motives behind a proposed deal?

_____

_____

_____

_____

_____

_____

_____

_____

_____

How will you assess your opponent's short- and longer-term goals (for the organization and the individual)?

_____

_____

_____

_____

_____

_____

_____

What will you do to assess your readiness to negotiate before the meeting?

_____

_____

_____

_____

_____

_____

_____

_____

_____

_____

3 PLANNING YOUR OBJECTIVES

 OUTCOMES FROM THIS CHAPTER

- Identify the motives behind a proposed deal.
- Understand explicit and implicit needs arising.
- Know the goals of both the organization and the individual.
- Analyse how decisions are made.
- Understand how to assess readiness to negotiate.
- Create a structured negotiating plan.

Are you the kind of person who goes shopping and realizes on returning home that you forgot to buy some of the items you needed? And, as you curse yourself for being such an idiot, do you remember how you silently made fun of the person alongside you at the supermarket patiently crossing items off on a list?

Regrettably, our memory power begins to decline from the age of 21 (which may also help to explain why we can so easily lose debates with our teenage children around the breakfast table!). As you will have seen from earlier chapters, there are few magic bullets that will enable us always to win disputes – or even come out of a negotiation with applause from our partners who have just conceded the debate to us.

To try to resolve this dilemma, most specialists will attempt to reconcile you to the best compromise. It's best for your planning and debate to focus on a win/win result because this is the one that will have most chance of satisfying everyone involved – and therefore will be implemented enthusiastically and stand the test of time.

🗩🗩 COACHING SESSION 26

Reflections on negotiating skills

Think about how you would measure your own skill as a negotiator. On the scale of 1 to 10, give yourself a score against the following criteria, with 10 being excellent and 1 poor.

Your personal rating	On a scale of 1 to 10
How effective am I?	
What's my track record?	
Have I had failures?	

1. How objective is this rating? Have you had client feedback or an appraisal, or simply guessed?

2. How could you find out?

3. If you don't know, who could you ask (without stimulating reactions/changes from your opponents)?

Now think about the skills of the person you are about to negotiate with.

Their personal rating	On a scale of 1 to 10
How effective are they?	
What's their track record?	
Have they had failures?	

4. If you don't know the answers to these questions, how could you find out?

5. How might you react if you find yourself having to negotiate with an opponent who you suspect has low ratings?

_____

_____

6. What actions would you take?

_____

_____

 COACH'S TIP

Think win/win

Anything less than a win/win will leave one of the parties feeling dissatisfied and so they may try to wreck the deal, even when they have signed up to it. Making deals collaborative – and conditional on implementation, as agreed – provides the best chance of success. But these things do not happen without careful thought and planning.

THE SKILLED NEGOTIATOR

Street bargaining is common in various parts of the world, and obviously involves negotiation, but the ways in which this is carried out are very different from business-to-business negotiation. The skills involved in business negotiation, while they will vary depending on the region or culture, the business climate and the nature of the industrial setting, usually focus on the need for care over the financial implications. The process itself pays attention to the characteristics of the individuals who create the deals. This is how it should be because, without those people, the deal probably wouldn't even have been thought of. Clearly, with practice and exposure – and bigger and better deals transacted – it would be natural for all those involved to start analysing the qualities of colleagues so that they can emulate the best qualities and skills of those negotiators who contributed to the deals.

 COACH'S TIP

Nurture relationships

Building relationships with people you have regular dealings with is more likely to lead to a partnering, co-operative relationship style, whereas 'one-off' deals with people you don't know can lead to competitive bargaining with a win/lose outcome.

BUILDING TRUST

An essential feature of the relationship between two negotiators is that of trust. Each party needs to be convinced that the deal that has been negotiated will be carried through exactly as agreed. While in the UK and some parts of Europe the preferred style is that of **win/win** (or **collaborative bargaining**), in some more relaxed environments (for example the Far East) a rather slower, **consensus style** tends to rule. This approach may feel long-winded to outsiders but it is felt essential that relationships be maintained – even to the extent that feelings are rarely 'tested' by disagreements. Outcomes, however, can still be win/win, win/lose or lose/lose.

Competitive negotiations tend to dominate commercial relationships in the Americas, which, again, may lead to a harsher style and generate some **win/lose** outcomes. In the UK there may be examples of all three styles in a round of negotiations – often driven by the style preferences of one or both negotiators.

COACH'S TIP

Use the 'if… then' formula

It is important that all negotiations should be conditional – that is, achieved by the use of the 'if… then' formula: 'If you supply that for me, then I'll promise to pay xx.' In other words, you exchange 'something for something'.

WHY NEGOTIATE?

Not so long ago, formal negotiation remained the province of powerful leaders of industries, politicians, trade union officials and international diplomats – at least, that's how many people saw it. Then we noticed that many of our partners didn't seem to play by the same rules as we did. It is a brave negotiator who tries to haggle in a street market in a foreign country unless accompanied by someone who can speak (or at least translate) the language. Because market traders are practised negotiators, driving a hard bargain every day over most things (if not everything), their skills are at a higher level than most people's.

In business, we negotiate because, if we do not, we may find ourselves paying too high a price and receiving a mediocre service or product with few enhancements, or we fail to exploit the real value of the product or service. This position is equally applicable to everyday living. We try negotiating with tradespeople and builders and often learn important lessons. When demand for a service is high, for example, such as after a storm when we and our neighbours all need our leaking roof to be mended, we learn that prices rise. Successful negotiation may involve forgetting about asking for a discount by simply getting on to your preferred supplier's list and achieving a completion date before the next storms arrive.

Similar principles apply in business-to-business negotiations, except that more subtleties may be applied. For example, inside knowledge about low demand affecting a particular car model is hinted at in the press – and a few local acres are rented to store the 'overflow'. The chance of a 'bargain deal' quickly becomes a 'target rumour' around the local community. (Such personal projects are valuable – because they provide good opportunities to polish your skills.)

Equally, you may wonder whether, for a quiet life, it is worth trying to negotiate at all. If this activity is not high on your list of priorities, it may colour your whole attitude to the skills and the commitment of both time and effort required. You may find the following coaching session helpful in strengthening both your motivation and personal profile towards negotiating – both in business and in your personal life.

⊇⊂ COACHING SESSION 27

Your personal negotiation profile

This exercise is designed to provide a starting point for an individual development plan – a kind of 'thermometer reading' of your current skills and, by implication, a potential stimulus for development. The questionnaire asks you to rate ten factors, each of which can make a contribution to achieving a successful deal or result.

For each statement, rate yourself on the scale of 1 to 7, depending on how much you agree with it.

	7	6	5	4	3	2	1	
Negotiation is co-operative.								Negotiation is competitive.
I seek a win.								I seek a fair deal.
My usual aim is a good result for both parties.								My usual aim is a good result for me.
I focus on the needs of my opponents.								I focus on the needs of my organization.
My opponents' needs often affect my objectives.								My opponents' needs never affect my objectives.

Measurable objectives are very important.								Measurable objectives are fairly important.
Both parties should be satisfied with the outcome.								Only one party needs to be satisfied with the outcome.
My power should be less than my opponents'.								My power should be more than my opponents'.
I prefer to negotiate on home ground.								I prefer to negotiate on the opponents' premises.
Targets are always planned on facts.								Targets are rarely planned on facts.
My commitment to targets is total.								My commitment to targets is fair.

A model marking scale for this exercise is included with the online resources for this chapter.

A STRUCTURED APPROACH: PROD-ProSC

Most tasks become easier and less intimidating when we have some guidelines to apply. This could be said to be true of cooking, changing the oil in the car, or preparing the departmental budget. Negotiation is no different!

As we have seen, this structured approach to the task of negotiation may be discarded during the negotiation itself. This is because, while skilled negotiators will apply a systematic approach to their *preparation*, the actual implementation may be much more flexible – and will therefore allow greater scope for the use of their skills and personality (and possibly charisma!). However, it is important that the style of the meeting does not overtake the progress and achievements to be gained by both sides.

This negotiation sequence is a framework to use when preparing for a specific case. Once you have made detailed preparations, you can move on to the likely stages involved in the meeting itself – discussed in later chapters.

As a reminder, the mnemonic PROD-ProSC stands for:

P = **Prepare**

▼

R = **Research**

▼

O = **Open**

▼

D = **Discuss and debate**

▼

Pro = **Propose**

▼

S = **Summarize**

▼

C = **Close**

Preparation: people

There is no doubt that people can be an important tactical resource in negotiation. We might all try to present the most likeable qualities in our personality to people we are trying to influence – and this will certainly make an effective contribution towards our negotiation goals. However, we also need to remember that our opponents are subjective human beings (just like us!) and they have their likes and dislikes about other people, which can obscure or obstruct progress towards objectives.

The first point to remember is that known inhibitions in the make-up of your opponent should be:

- researched
- planned for
- dealt with.

In this way you can minimize any negative effects. This could include recasting negotiator roles if, for example, you discover that your opponent would prefer to deal with a woman (or, perhaps, a man). It could also be that they will be more respectful of an opponent with some grey hair rather than, say, a recent graduate – or the reverse.

Within the constraints of hierarchy, it is generally best to field the most persuasive negotiator – especially when there are known preferences. This advice might not meet our preferences for an equal and egalitarian society, but that should be a separate agenda item for a different discussion elsewhere. Negotiators should not confuse their agenda objectives in such meetings.

COACH'S TIP

Meet expectations

However we may resist the thought, failure to pay attention to the expectations of the other party can result in the loss of an important deal.

Preparation: presentation style

Some people play on their appearance or presentation style in order to intimidate their opponents. For example, a large person can sometimes present him- or herself in an aggressive way in the sure knowledge that the departmental team (or, maybe, union membership?) will not argue with such intimidation.

This effect can be gained from:

- physical size – emphasized by unrestrained gestures(!)
- a loud voice
- a hectoring manner
- a 'larger-than-life' personality.

Such concerns may affect the choice of lead negotiator but should not affect the use of best technique and skills in the meetings – especially if emotive issues are involved.

COACHING SESSION 28

Improving your presentation style

Think about the following aspects of your style of presentation and how it might appear to others. Jot down your ideas.

Your use of language

_____

_____

_____

Your personal appearance

_____

_____

_____

Your general demeanour (e.g, positive, persuasive, prepared, people-oriented)

_____

_____

Your command of the facts (e.g. researched, in control of market intelligence)

_____

_____

Which 'allies' could help you develop these factors where needed?

_____

_____

Research

Better deals are undoubtedly achievable and the level of effort devoted to research and preparation can make a big difference. A negotiator who has prepared the case thoroughly and _knows what has been agreed elsewhere_ will have a distinct advantage over average negotiators who have not completed research to uncover this knowledge. It is not just that they are more confident: it is also that more pressurized arguments can be applied to secure a more advantageous deal.

 COACH'S TIP

Good research makes better deals

Better deals should result from investing more effort in research.

How can we undertake better research?

Most organizations take steps to ensure that key decisions or strategies are coded 'Company Confidential' and, by implication, are prepared to impose the ultimate sanction against anyone who reveals all. This may not stop 'leaks', however. Whenever employees leave an organization, knowledge goes with them, and this is how many people enhance their 'market worth' in the first place. An important and sizeable deal may be influenced considerably by nuggets of information that are obtainable from a former (or a dissatisfied) employee.

A great deal of useful information about *current* trading conditions can also often be obtained from casual conversations with present (possibly lower-level) employees. Such people may not have been briefed on how to behave with outsiders and may be a valuable source of 'native intelligence'. It is amazing how helpful cleaners, drivers, receptionists, post workers and service technicians can be! Quite aside from this kind of investigation, skilled negotiators will ensure that they are armed with the most up-to-date facts about the marketplace in which they are working and this is where the specialist can score above the occasional operator.

In this respect, buyers and sellers who are in the fast-moving consumer goods markets have a currency that is extremely valuable to competitors. Once a negotiator is out of touch for any length of time (e.g. through redundancy or illness), past experience may have become out of date and considerable research may be needed to succeed with a re-entry into the market.

 COACH'S TIP

Keep up to date

Knowledge of the current rate for recent deals is extremely valuable in the negotiation process – making win/win deals easier and quicker to achieve.

Here's a checklist of questions to ask to help drive your research needs:

1. What customs exist:
   i. in this business sector?
   ii. with this opponent?
2. How much power do they carry?
3. Who might have influence with/over them (e.g. press/trade bodies)?
4. What is their dominant business culture?
5. Who would be their final authority?
6. What is the influence of time/timing/place?
7. What is the evidence of their:
   i. deadlock handling?
   ii. use of fixed solutions?
   iii. closed statements (e.g. 'You must accept that...')?
   iv. emotional outbursts?

    v. lack of follow-through (e.g. promises made but not fulfilled)?

   vi. creditworthiness/fluidity?

  vii. buoyancy of market/business strength?

 viii. market position (e.g. dominance)?

   ix. earlier issues likely to be resurrected?

    x. predominant negotiation style (e.g. high/low reactor; patience; determination; principled)?

◯◯ COACHING SESSION 29

Your specific needs for the deal

Think about what further criteria may be relevant to your specific sector.

1. List them here.

_____

_____

_____

_____

_____

2. If these were provided by a senior colleague, when were they last reviewed?

_____

_____

3. How up to date are they?

_____

_____

4. Do you fully understand their importance and relevance to your project(s)?

_____

_____

Early stages checklist

Check the following points and add your notes to your action plan in the appendix.

Questions and issues	Answers
P = Prepare	
a) People? Who am I meeting? What authority do they have? Who else is likely to be present? What do we know about the culture and style of this organization/ business and, particularly, the people who run it?	
ITEMS NEEDED	
b) Documentation?	
c) Samples?	
d) Notes on client?	
e) Illustrations of service to others?	

ONLINE RESOURCE

Early stages checklist

Find a copy of this checklist in the online resources for Chapter 2, where you first encountered it. Print it out and use as a prompt when preparing for future meetings. Go to:

www.TYCoachbooks.com/Negotiation

PLANNING THE MEETING

The PROD-ProSC formula provides a valuable framework for us to use in 'set-piece' negotiations, but will it always work? Unlike other management behaviours, better negotiation results are generally obtainable when all the players are equally well trained. In other words, one side or the other may gain a limited advantage but the overall aim should be for a 'quality win' – one that benefits all parties.

Failure to adopt a sequenced approach to the meeting does not necessarily indicate an untrained negotiator. It may point to a deliberate attempt to form an individual style or gain some tactical advantage and, when coupled with the exercise of a charismatic personality, the result can be extraordinarily effective. So, while the logical approach to the meeting may appear to be the best (or only) method to adopt, the reader should always be alert to unstructured approaches and develop the ability to use or respond to these, too.

COACH'S TIP

Copy the chess grand masters

Chess grand masters spend large periods of their life trying to out-think the strategies of their opponents – with a very large prize at stake. The enthusiastic negotiator could do worse than emulate this example.

Here is the step-by-step approach to planning:

1. Identify your own organization's needs.
2. Prioritize or rank those needs according to short-term versus long-term factors.
3. Identify your options for setting limits and satisfying needs from most favourable to least favourable positions.
4. Identify the possible needs of the opponent.
5. Prioritize the exploration of options (and rank the opponent's options).

6. Identify the opponent's options (and seek common ground).

7. Compare both sets of options.

8. Establish common ground.

9. Prepare each issue individually.

10. Brief any colleagues likely to be attending the meeting.

Digging for detail

When it comes to the main task – seeking objectives (which may overlap) for the forthcoming meeting – the following format is helpful in ensuring that preparation is as thorough as possible. All the elements of the plan will need to be completed in advance (with any gaps to be explored in the meeting itself). This process is called 'digging for detail' because some data may be difficult (if not impossible) to chart, and you may need to make estimates, based on:

- individual research

- limited/educated forecasting

- past experience.

The objectives model

In a commercial setting, objectives for flexible price setting (for example) may be described as 'banded' along the following continuum:

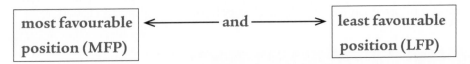

This is where the buyer's position is the reverse of the seller's. When the asking price is clear (from price lists, quotes, etc.), each person's bottom line needs to be assessed. Exactly the same principle can be made to apply to an employee relations case. (The online resources for this chapter include a provocative element suggesting that a 'going rate' may not always be the best starting point for this prepared model.)

The following example is from the buyer's position. The objectives themselves are prioritized using the MIL formula:

- **M** = I must achieve

- **I** = I intend to achieve

- **L** = I would like to achieve (but this is not essential)

Planning sheet for objectives

Our shopping list					Their shopping list
1. PRICE (buyer)	US most favourable (MFP)	£72,000–£77,500	least favourable (LFP)		PRICE (seller)
	least favourable	£72,500–£80,000	most favourable THEM		
2. QUANTITY	US MFP			LFP	QUANTITY (seller)
	LFP			MFP THEM	
3. PAYMENT TERMS	US MFP			LFP	TERMS (seller)
	LFP			MFP THEM	
4. PROMOTION SUPPORT	US MFP			LFP	SUPPORT (seller)
	LFP			MFP THEM	

Clearly, some details may be difficult, initially, to project – but the advantage of this format is that it provides a real baseline from which experiences, conversations, other deals and opportunities will reinforce the negotiator's confidence to seek better terms from the opponent. In other words, new proposals will be formed from research based on known deals that others have achieved elsewhere.

 **ONLINE RESOURCE**

Planning sheet

A further completed example of this planning sheet is in the online resources for this chapter, which also include a blank template that you can print off and use for your own meeting planning. Go to:

www.TYCoachbooks.com/Negotiation

MFP/LFP: a plan for failure or flexibility?

So far we have made the assumption that, once a negotiation is opened and arguments voiced, movement in positions will occur and that, eventually, a mutually acceptable deal will arrive. But whose 'acceptable' is acceptable?

A vital part of the plan has to be the pitching of the figures (or positions) that are:

- best (gold-star)
- good (silver)
- acceptable (bronze)
- unacceptable (below the 'red line').

In reality, we are describing a continuum of (mainly) numbers that have been subjected to scrutiny and rating for acceptability by each negotiator's organization. This element is essential to avoid the risk of the negotiators agreeing to a plan that is subsequently rejected by a more senior manager. (This unfortunate result can occur when a negotiator is accountable but total authority has been withheld.)

For simplicity, we are proposing two positions: those that are most favourable (MFP) and those that are least favourable (LFP).

Now we can see the vital task played by preparation – it's not just working out *our* needs but also accounting for values from:

- **past deals** that proved unprofitable (i.e. unacceptable)
- **successful deals** that have made a good contribution to current targets
- **'vote-winning' deals** that have been significant as they have generated outstanding results and built up partnerships with clients or suppliers.

For each agenda item, it is essential to apply the labels **MFP** and **LFP** so that the bands of acceptability can guide the negotiator towards satisfactory points of balance during discussion and bargaining.

COACH'S TIP

Use the quid pro quo

What about items that are not flexible (e.g. a unique antique picture)? A price may be agreed at auction but there is little outside this for a supplier to offer – except, perhaps, professional delivery at a flexible cost level and/or a comprehensive insurance package. In commercial sectors, non-flexible elements are sometimes used as exchangeable items: 'You do this for me and I'll do that for you', or quid pro quo.

Critics (probably mostly competitive negotiators) would say that, even thinking about fallback positions (LFPs) already suggests that a negotiator is accepting defeat – not really expecting to win agreement on all the most favourable positions. (Could this be why some extremely competitive people find negotiating difficult?)

PLANNING STRATEGIES AND TACTICS

Before moving ahead with the practical implementation of the plan, it would be good to review your proposed strategies and tactics.

COACHING SESSION 30

Looking at client reactions

Here is a checklist for reviewing the BuGS/SOS case study as described so far. Any gaps you uncover would need to be fully researched and recorded for the players' personal action plans for progress before the next meeting.

1. What was the client's reaction to the proposition? How weak or strong is their need for the proposals?

2. What are the benefits that will condition their actual stance?

3. What problems do they have?

4. What are 'our' problems?

5. How can these be best identified and reconciled?

6. What pressures exist for them to conclude a deal now, or later?

7. How are they likely to express the strength of their need (bearing in mind what points we have)?

_____

_____

8. How could we raise the value of these (i.e. cheap for us but valuable to them?)

_____

_____

9. What concessions could we reasonably expect from them?

_____

_____

10. How might these compare with our bargaining points?

_____

_____

11. Who is likely to be present at the next meeting? (What do we know about them – i.e. authority, style, tactics, strength? How could we find out more?)

_____

_____

_____

_____

ADVANCED CHALLENGES

Rather more complicated (and potentially difficult) are those negotiations that involve:

- political issues
- strategic choices
- long-term factors
- matters of principle
- 'what-if' issues
- international applications (e.g. common language/interpretation).

Any (or all) of these are likely to require much more time and effort in research and preparation before any meetings are arranged.

ΩΩ COACHING SESSION 31

Objectives planning

Bearing in mind your recent/current negotiation experiences and the need for thorough preparation, rate yourself against each of the following criteria (circle the number that applies, with 7 being 'Always' and 1 'Never').

Do I:	Rating
Allow my opponents to do most of the talking in the early stages?	7 6 5 4 3 2 1
Always have the relevant facts and figures to hand?	7 6 5 4 3 2 1
Avoid emotional reactions – but satisfy opponents' emotional needs?	7 6 5 4 3 2 1
Allow opponents to save face in granting a concession?	7 6 5 4 3 2 1
Move from opening stated stances to a clear statement of actual stances, taking care to condition the concessions on both sides?	7 6 5 4 3 2 1
Avoid too firm a stance on any point that might result in reaching a point of no return too soon?	7 6 5 4 3 2 1
Maintain a non-committal stance if facing one of my proposals being refused?	7 6 5 4 3 2 1
Use a 'trial close' on a clear statement of the actual gap between you?	7 6 5 4 3 2 1
Value concessions thoroughly so you can raise their value to your opponent above their real cost to you?	7 6 5 4 3 2 1
Trade concessions one at a time?	7 6 5 4 3 2 1
If complete agreement is impossible, ensure that the door is kept open so that each side is able to go back, consult and renegotiate after seeking clarification on points of disagreement?	7 6 5 4 3 2 1

Now compare your ratings with the scores given in the online resource for this coaching session.

Then reconsider each of the factors listed above and note down what preparations you would have to make in order to apply each of these principles. (A model answer is contained in the online resource.)

ONLINE RESOURCE

Planning checklist

Taking a current example from your own workplace, complete the planning checklist included in the online resource, which should help identify some key issues and challenges that may require more advanced techniques and skills. Go to:

www.TYCoachbooks.com/Negotiation

REVIEW CHECKLIST

Before rushing to your meeting, ask yourself these final questions:

1. Have I established the MFPs and LFPs?

2. Have I prepared a strategy for obtaining movement?

3. Am I prepared to move from the starting position?

4. Could any issues be linked together (i.e. exchanged)?

5. Could I use hypothetical arguments (e.g. 'Supposing we...')?

6. Do I have an adjournment strategy?

7. Could sanctions be applied as part of the bargaining process?

8. How do the parties view the need to bargain fairly?

PROD-ProSC

Your current stage on the map is highlighted in bold.

Stage	Issues
P = Prepare a) People b) Place	 What do I know about the culture and style of representatives of this business/organization? How affected am I likely to be by the personal comfort factors – e.g. distractions, noise and interruptions, seating/layout?
R = Research and planning	**What is our opponents' position?** **Motives? Needs? Goals?** **Who are the key authorizing players?** **Negotiating plan gained from advance identification of:** • **motives lying behind a proposed deal** • **explicit and implicit needs arising** • **short- and longer-term goals (organizational and for the individual)** • **analysis of authority (i.e. how decisions are made) so that readiness can be assessed prior to attending the meeting.**
O = Open	How should I open the meeting? What ice-breaking topics might be used? Are there any probing questions I could ask? How could we establish some common ground?
D = Discuss and debate	What style of conversation should I adopt?
Pro = Propose (Conflict management)	How will I resist the temptation to move too quickly/slowly? What if we disagree in a major way?
S = Summarize	How good am I at using summaries in meetings?
C = Close	What methods of closing can I use most effectively?

Once you have explored your current stage, note in your action plan any areas that might need more attention.

NEXT STEPS

You should now have sufficient support to enable you to prepare a structured negotiating plan gained from advance identification of:

1 the motives behind a proposed deal

2 explicit and implicit needs arising

3 short- and longer-term goals – organizational and for the individual

4 analysis of authority.

The next chapter is about setting up the meeting itself, taking account of the factors that can affect how decisions are made and other influences on the outcome. From this you will be able to assess your readiness for the negotiation to take place.

TAKEAWAYS

How committed are you to making changes to your negotiating in order to gain improved results? Give some positive examples that illustrate your motivation and determination.

_____

_____

_____

_____

_____

_____

_____

_____

If/when you are challenged with obstructions/objections/hazards, do you normally:

a) fight harder?
b) research alternative approaches?
c) give up (rationalizing that things are as they are for a reason)?
d) work harder to gain success by rethinking your approach?

_____

_____

_____

_____

Explain why you adopt this approach.

_____

_____

_____

_____

Given your circumstances, is there a better option? If not, what should you do about it and who might be able to help?

_____

_____

_____

_____

_____

Most change involves these challenges, so what else can you do to buttress your objectives and aspirations?

_____

_____

_____

_____

Who do you know (at work or in your social group) who could act as your mentor in buttressing your determination by listening to your experimentations and results (while retaining confidentiality in your business)?

_____

_____

_____

_____

_____

_____

4 | SETTING UP YOUR MEETING

✔ OUTCOMES FROM THIS CHAPTER

- Understand authority and how decisions are made.
- Know your personal skills and preferences for using persuasion.
- Know how to take account of your 'opponent' and the preferred location for the negotiation.
- Identify the 'unknowns' that can affect the outcome of the discussion.
- Know how to limit the potentially negative influencing power of environment, conversational tactics, interruptions and crises.
- Assess readiness for attending the negotiation meeting.

The *Oxford Dictionary* defines negotiation as:

'Some meeting and expression of views (i.e. "confer") with another (i.e. two or more persons) in which there may be disagreement, but that there is an intention to reach agreement (i.e. through compromise)'.

This definition makes the whole process seem a great deal simpler than it often appears to be in practice. We have already described the important factors that can affect the outcome of our meetings and in this chapter we look at some measures of success related to the people involved in the negotiation and the location of the meeting.

A successful negotiator is one who:

- is rated as effective by *both* sides
- has a track record of significant success
- has a low incidence of implementation failure.

TO MEET OR NOT TO MEET?

We should not assume that we *have* to meet in order to negotiate successfully. There are, of course, many advantages to a physical meeting (especially the opportunity it provides to observe and 'read' the body language of your opponent), but sometimes this is just not possible and yet negotiations can still reach successful outcomes and implementation.

COACHING SESSION 32

Measuring success

1. How would you measure the success of a negotiation?

2. How do you think your opponent would measure *their* success?

3. Are your answers very different? And, if so, why is this?

4. What quality in the relationship would you say is essential to a successful negotiation?

Pressure and pace of business have led to short cuts in the ways in which we might wish to conduct our business. We could use the telephone or telex, exchange written communications (snail mail or email) or we could make use of the sheer speed and delivery of video conferencing and even social media (including Facebook and Twitter).

The critical feature of deals made between negotiators who have never met is trust. (Trust may take years to build up but can be broken in the blink of an eye – or one simple mistake on the invoice – and the results can be extremely costly.) How can trust be developed between people who have never met?

Meetings are very common in business – but the more people who attend them the more costly they are (in time) and it could also be said that, often, 'less is more'. While a physical meeting with everyone in the same room has several advantages, the more people there are in a meeting means the less everyone can speak – and so decisions can be more difficult to achieve when a large number of people attend a meeting. This means that, when considering who should be involved, we should consider output as well as input.

🗩🗩 COACHING SESSION 33

Communication methods

Against the following list of communication methods, write in your list of advantages and disadvantages of that method if it were the *sole method of communicating* with your opponent for an important negotiation.

Method	Advantages	Disadvantages
Telephone		
Email		
Texting		
Letter		
Social media		
Telex/fax		
Physical meeting		

Arranging a meeting may seem like the natural way of progressing a negotiation, but face-to-face discussion brings risks as well as advantages. Some people are habitual talkers (it's easier than working, isn't it?!). Others may be 'loners' with poor social skills – preferring their own company and thoughts to those of their opponents. Neither provides a good starting point for using your persuasion skills.

CULTURES OF NEGOTIATION

Negotiation takes place in different 'cultures' – and these are strongly affected by the nationality, territorial and organizational climate of those involved.

There are three widely recognized styles of interaction:

1. **Competitive (win/lose)**

   Commonly associated and sourced from the USA or American-trained negotiators, this, put crudely, is a 'first-past-the-post' concept – and is easy if you have market domination and don't need to be concerned with building partnerships. Negotiators are vulnerable to competitive strategies with one-off deals – where competitive negotiators might consider it unnecessary to worry about repeat business or how their opponents view them.

2. **Consensual (win/win or lose/lose)**

   Mainly emanating from the Far East, this style emphasizes the relationship and face-saving aspects of negotiation. It can be relatively slow to achieve results.

3. **Collaborative (win/win)**

   This may be the style that most Europeans are familiar with.

An essential element in preparing to negotiate is therefore establishing which of these climates or cultures is likely to dominate the atmosphere in which the negotiation will take place.

Whatever negotiating style you face, it is essential to focus on ensuring that all negotiation utilizes the 'conditional approach'; this is achieved by using the formula 'if...then'. This approach helps to condition all parties to the idea that movement and concessions should be two-way. Failure to apply this approach may play into the hands of a competitive negotiator who is naturally inclined towards a win/lose result.

 COACH'S TIP

Use the conditional approach

'If you do this for us… then we'll do that for you!' provides a much better chance of building successful partnerships.

Understanding culture

When we think about the new people we are going to meet, it is important to prepare for the probable culture that may be dominant in their psychological make-up. 'Culture' here goes beyond nationality, original home territory and industrial application and relates to broader issues of outlook and general assumptions. This needs to be a cautious but thorough process and it would be most valuable if you can draw on someone else's experience – for example, someone inside your organization who has negotiated with these opponents before. This might be:

- a trusted and confidential third party

- a commentator with some inside knowledge of the opponent's organization.

COACH'S TIP

Don't make judgements

Take care not to dilute your credibility by giving your opponent the impression of naivety or mistrust of their culture.

If you are a person who prefers to talk first and plan afterwards (or maybe just to talk without too much of a worry about making false judgements), you may need no encouragement to meet to negotiate. If you are fortunate enough to have maintained excellent and consistent results from your current approach, then stay as you are! For the rest of us, the need to prepare properly helps us to avoid being overwhelmed by those with charismatic personalities and persuasive skills that are well above average. Fun though you might find negotiating (and it can be!), it can still be extremely time-consuming, nerve-jangling and draining intellectually. So, unless there are hidden motives, the best advice is to negotiate only when you have to.

THE BENEFITS OF MEETINGS

Negotiation, by its very nature, is about creating and agreeing to a change that will be implemented. This is easy to say for the people who are seeking the change, but others may find reasons (and excuses) for not agreeing to it. You may find that the other party is:

- **vacillating** about even the need to meet to discuss change

- **ascribing low priority** to the need

- agreeing the need but **delaying** making meeting arrangements

- **putting off implementation** after agreement has been reached.

This can be frustrating for anyone whose time is precious and who wants to move projects forward. On its own, arranging a meeting does not solve these challenges but it should be possible for an experienced negotiator to assess in one meeting whether agreement and change is ever likely to occur. By careful and precise questioning, it is possible to assess needs and (as salespeople are taught) to 'qualify' your opponent. This will benefit both parties equally and help save time and energy.

The principal benefit of a meeting over other methods (if the opportunity is taken properly) is that the occasion is interactive – involving the exchange of information – and ideas and proposals can be tested in conversation. Critical to all this is the understanding, on both sides, that there is authority on both sides to commit their organizations to a deal. As we have seen – and know from experience – most negotiators are fully trustworthy and do not make promises they cannot keep. Sadly, this is not always the case and promises may be made (e.g. by telephone or in a message exchange) but not kept. It is less easy to commit to such behaviour when your preferred approach is a face-to-face meeting.

A meeting has the advantage of allowing you to observe and interpret body language, which gives a 'third dimension' to communicating. While this is quite a study in itself, it is relatively easy to spot some common behaviours indicating:

- uncertainty about the information given
- discomfort of the speaker (if, for example, they are giving information that is known or suspected to be inaccurate).

A trained observer should be able to pick up such signals and take a more circumspect approach as a result.

WHO SHOULD ATTEND?

Attending a negotiation meeting could result in an agreement that will commit all parts of an organization to an action. Such actions could involve making changes to:

- forward investment
- volume of goods
- purchases of components or raw materials
- number and types of employees and/or machines
- subcontractors' services
- authority and permissions (e.g. for planning)
- forward pricing.

It is only reasonable that the other parties to an agreement can trust that we have the authority inside our own organization to commit to a deal. This could imply a considerable level of authority – and freedom to make that decision. In reality, many negotiations are conducted on the assumption that a third party – who may not be present – is the real authority and that, until he or she is present to sign, all other agreements are purely provisional. So, what happens if basic agreement is reached at the first stage – but the final authority is not satisfied and agreement is withheld? Such a situation is neither desirable nor helpful – and the negotiators might well feel like resigning!

The best solution is to ensure that the 'signing authority' is a key member of the negotiation – and/or progress is staged so that he/she is always in control (behind the scenes) by maintaining close communication with the negotiators. Clearly, this assumes open access and excellent two-way briefing.

 COACH'S TIP

Check authority levels

As a negotiator, it is obviously critical to establish not only that you have the authority to reach agreement but to find out (diplomatically) whether or not your opposite number also has the authority to negotiate on behalf of their organization.

In reality, most established organizations are experienced in maintaining management systems and levels of authority to guide their negotiators – and the only time when they need to intervene is when an important point of principle is reached. An often-quoted reason for making face-to-face negotiations an essential part of an organization's strategy is that trust can be judged and tested by observing the non-verbal behaviour of the opponent.

Meetings provide a greater chance of influencing an outcome than remoter communication because they give a 'stage' on which negotiators may 'perform' and exploit their personalities. Such occasions also provide great opportunities for you to observe and analyse the body language of your opponents – looking for inconsistencies and any discomfort arising from less than full and frank disclosures. However, while non-verbal behaviour provides valuable supporting evidence, it can also be subjective and notoriously open to interpretation.

 COACH'S TIP

Limit the size of the meeting

Notwithstanding the above comments, negotiating meetings should normally aim to include as few people as possible (on the 'need to know' basis). Large meetings risk loss of control – and negotiators 'playing to the audience'. Inevitably, they are also much more expensive.

⏹⏹ COACHING SESSION 34

Assessing your non-verbal behaviour skills

The purpose of this questionnaire is for you to highlight your behaviours and habits that may have an impact on the people around you. Complete the questionnaire by circling the number on the scale you feel applies to your behaviour and present skills – where 1 means 'Rarely' and 6 means 'Often' – especially as they occur in your negotiation meetings. When you have completed this exercise in private, ask someone who knows you well to check your scoring for accuracy – from their knowledge/observations of you.

I am a person who...	Rating
1 Likes to listen to other people talk	1 2 3 4 5 6
2 Encourages others to talk	1 2 3 4 5 6
3 Listens well to friends	1 2 3 4 5 6
4 Listens well to acquaintances and family	1 2 3 4 5 6
5 Behaves in an uninhibited way in all situations	1 2 3 4 5 6
6 Copies other people's behaviour in meetings	1 2 3 4 5 6
7 Resists other people's attempts to influence me	1 2 3 4 5 6
8 Controls my own non-verbal behaviour	1 2 3 4 5 6
9 Observes other people's behaviour	1 2 3 4 5 6
10 Talks through one/both hands	1 2 3 4 5 6
11 Uses a firm handshake on meeting	1 2 3 4 5 6
12 Maintains strong eye contact during conversations	1 2 3 4 5 6
13 Uses a relaxed/laid-back posture	1 2 3 4 5 6
14 Leaves off tasks/reading to talk or listen to others	1 2 3 4 5 6
15 Looks at the speaker	1 2 3 4 5 6
16 Ignores distractions while talking/listening	1 2 3 4 5 6
17 Smiles/nods/encourages the speaker to talk	1 2 3 4 5 6
18 Thinks about what I'm told	1 2 3 4 5 6
19 Uses hand/arm gestures during speech	1 2 3 4 5 6
20 Plays with a pen/calculator, etc. during a conversation	1 2 3 4 5 6
21 Folds my arms when listening	1 2 3 4 5 6
22 Discloses my emotions readily through facial expressions	1 2 3 4 5 6
23 Observes facial feedback/reaction to my talk	1 2 3 4 5 6
24 Imitates the other person's posture	1 2 3 4 5 6
25 Controls uninhibited behaviour in conversation	1 2 3 4 5 6
26 Tries to understand the speaker's meaning	1 2 3 4 5 6
27 Tries to understand *why* the speaker is communicating	1 2 3 4 5 6

28 Lets the speaker finish what he/she is saying	1 2 3 4 5 6
29 Encourages the speaker to finish if he/she hesitates	1 2 3 4 5 6
30 Restates what is said to check understanding	1 2 3 4 5 6
31 Experiences uncertainty in speech (ums and ers)	1 2 3 4 5 6
32 Uses silence in conversations	1 2 3 4 5 6
33 Is insulated against the irritators/fidgeting of speakers	1 2 3 4 5 6
34 Observes others' willingness to hear out a long speech by watching their eye gaze	1 2 3 4 5 6
35 Moves away/closer when listening	1 2 3 4 5 6
36 Runs hand through hair while talking	1 2 3 4 5 6
37 Rubs palms together when listening/speaking	1 2 3 4 5 6
38 Witholds judgement until a speaker has finished	1 2 3 4 5 6
39 Listens to ideas – not the manner or choice of words	1 2 3 4 5 6
40 Listens, even when the next words/ideas can be anticipated	1 2 3 4 5 6
41 Asks the speaker to define/explain technical/unfamiliar words	1 2 3 4 5 6

When you have completed this task, check the online resources for Chapter 4 and compare your ratings with the ideal answers for this task, adding your findings to your action plan.

NON-VERBAL COMMUNICATION

Non-verbal behaviour includes a wide range of elements that transmit attitudes and emotions during all communications. Skilled negotiators are sensitive to the non-verbal behaviour of their opponents and are able to reinforce their negotiating tactics by the conscious use of various non-verbal signals.

Facial expressions

Strategies in negotiation may lead negotiators to control the extent to which they reveal, for example:

- interest in a particular product or suggestion
- surprise about an opponent's offer
- happiness with the overall deal.

The mouth and eyebrows are the areas that disclose the most information about a person's feelings.

Gestures

Gestures are often used to emphasize particular parts of the communication and may also, unconsciously, reveal the emotional state of the negotiator; for example:

- face-touching may indicate anxiety
- clenched fists may indicate aggression
- suppression of 'natural' hand gestures or nose-touching may indicate deceit.

Posture

It may also be important to note the posture of communicators during negotiations; apart from anything else, it may reveal the extent to which the negotiator is relaxed. There may be occasions when one negotiator imitates the posture of the other (e.g. sitting with legs crossed). This usually indicates a level of friendship between two people, although the dominant person may also use it to help put the other person at ease.

Shifts of gaze

Making eye contact is often associated with sincerity and honesty, while frequent shifts of gaze are associated with 'shiftiness' and distrust. The eyes provide vital information about where the other person is looking and with what expression. You can learn a lot by observing:

- blink rate
- the extent to which the person's eyes are open
- overall facial expression
- where the person looks after they move their gaze from the other person's face.

All these elements will give you information about:

- the effect on them of what another person is currently saying (e.g. smiling, frowning, laughing)
- the person's willingness to hear the speaker out (especially during a long speech)
- the degree of acceptance of what is being said.

Non-verbal aspects of speech

This includes 'ums' and 'ers', tone of voice and long pauses. Effective negotiation is usually positive in tone, with fewer hesitant speech patterns than a less effective negotiation, when hesitancy (including 'ums' and 'ers') may indicate uncertainty, insecurity or deceit.

Silence and long pauses can help to inject tension into a negotiation. This tactic may be used with great success by an effective negotiator who may put pressure on their opponent by simply waiting for a reply to a proposal. (This is especially important when you are trying to close a deal without having to make last-minute concessions.)

COACHING SESSION 35

Observing non-verbal communication

Watch a current-affairs discussion programme on TV and record the behaviour of the participants (including the chairperson) using the observation chart from the previous coaching session.

To avoid overload and confusion, aim for groups of just ten factors from the listing at a time. This task is more effective if you can carry it out with one or two colleagues – this enables analysis and discussion of your interpretations.

CONSIDERING THE VENUE

The idea that the venue for a negotiating meeting might affect its outcome may seem absurd. However, most people have strong preferences (not all of them conscious ones) and personal physical or psychological comfort can greatly affect a meeting.

Consider the options. Do you prefer to negotiate 'at home' or 'away'? Either option provides strengths and weaknesses, opportunities and threats. Many managers prefer to meet on their home territory because it gives them the opportunity to manage the meeting, have control over the physical factors (such as interruptions, distractions, tidiness of surroundings) and to provide refreshments – all of which can help the meeting go as they planned.

On the other hand, marketers will often draw attention to the great advantage of 'playing away', which potentially provides many additional learning opportunities. For example, you can observe the strengths and weaknesses of the other side, such as:

- the condition of the building (and vehicles outside it)
- the demeaning way in which an apparently senior executive may be hectored

- how often your meeting is interrupted
- your opponent's ability to cope with paperwork.

Much of this might seem unimportant – and to skilled negotiators it should be. However, confidence in negotiation meetings is vital and the slightest discomfort can make a difference when the pressure is on. For example, a meeting being held in the middle of a retail selling department – where samples are being considered by a buyer while retail customers are also browsing nearby – may intimidate either buyer or seller because discussions of cost prices and margins need to be kept from the customers. In this situation, which of the players is more likely to be discomforted?

An obvious alternative could be to arrange to meet on neutral territory, which suggests that both sides are put at the same disadvantage. This might sound fair, but a hotel or conference centre might turn out to be an extension of 'home territory' for the suggesting partner – who then may gain some subtle advantage from being known and supported by the management and staff at the venue.

Sometimes a negotiation is conducted in the hosts' showroom, which almost certainly is a carefully managed environment – or should be. This should not make any difference to an experienced operator, who may welcome the additional challenge. The initiator may in fact gain false confidence from feeling that they are 'playing a home game'.

Factors to consider when deciding on a venue include:

- predictability vs unpredictability (more or less relaxing)
- confidentiality vs lack of confidentiality (will you be overheard?)
- levels of comfort and support
- distractions.

EXTERNAL NEGOTIATIONS

The atmosphere and culture of a negotiation will feel different according to which side you are on.

The seller's perspective

There is a presumption by most negotiators that the correct venue for a sales negotiation is the buyers' venue. This presumption is based on the concept that the 'persuader' should expect to go to the buyer. However, negotiations may take place at a trade fair, over a lunch or in a hotel meeting room. What is true is that the atmosphere at such a meeting, wherever it is held, is likely to be characterized by sellers who are extrovert and using their skills to promote their firm and its products to achieve a sales result. We would be surprised if the salesperson could not do that enthusiastically. But the targets should not just be a large order: the buyer will be expecting competent advice and post-sales support (e.g. prompt delivery and trouble-free invoicing), while the supplier will be expecting payment on time in accordance with the terms and conditions.

Successful commercial salespeople also know that it is important to satisfy buyers' needs to:

- avoid risk, trouble and unnecessary work
- gain support at times of trouble
- feel competent
- make difficult decisions
- have their voice heard
- avoid learning about changes in a supplier's organization second-hand
- be thought of as fair and 'nice'.

By contrast, sales teams must also:

- achieve sales targets
- gain recognition for their expertise, technical knowledge and advice
- socialize
- be successful and contribute to the long-term success of their company.

The best relationships are those that develop into partnerships, since neither side can truly succeed without the other. Negotiations are likely to reach deals based on exchange of concessions – for example, a small discount earned from a slight change in quantities ordered – and it may take some time for a balance to be struck and agreed. Ultimately, the real test of a lasting relationship will be the goodwill arising from successful repeating contracts. The seller aims to:

- make deals and trade concessions in small steps – and slowly
- emphasize the long-term value and security of the deal
- defend price by emphasis on service, quality, security, long-term investment, etc.
- make the buyer work hard for concessions (to avoid being seen as a pushover).

The buyer's perspective

Buyers need to seek an equitable price and will be prepared to be flexible, provided that other factors are in balance. They need to see:

- price matched with quality
- good availability

- reliable deliveries
- a specification suitable for their needs
- proof of value and reputation (e.g. the 'brand')
- costs in real terms
- effective technical backup and support.

INTERNAL NEGOTIATIONS

All the principles considered so far also apply to negotiations across departments or divisions of your own organization. For example, they apply to 'service' departments such as:

- Sales Support (i.e. promotion and presentation)
- Finance and Accounting
- Work Study and Efficiency
- Human Resources
- Transport
- Market Research.

These departments will all have plans that will affect service continuity of the executing functions of the business or organization – and negotiations will be necessary when their plans have a direct impact on work there. If such changes are implemented without proper consultation and involvement, the result can be disruption or even outright conflict. Forward involvement and sensitive consultation and negotiation will help avoid these outcomes.

 COACH'S TIP

Keep your goal in mind

With most, if not all, negotiated settlements, the ultimate goal is to achieve success in all deals and to maintain lasting goodwill. Therefore, you should always avoid deals based on short-term gain or on claims that later turn out to be false. The priority is to maintain your reputation for credibility and integrity.

QQ COACHING SESSION 36

Planning your venue

Test out the principles of this chapter at a forthcoming negotiation. Use the spaces below to write down your plan for the venue.

1. Where will you meet?

2. Home or away?

3. What are the advantages?

4. What are the disadvantages?

5. What is the meeting room layout like?

6. Are any adjustments necessary/possible? If so, how?

7. What is the seating comfort like?

8. How will I manage interruptions and other potential 'power games'?

9. How can I make the communications work for me?

_____

_____

10. Are there any personal comfort factors to consider?

_____

_____

11. How affected am I likely to be by the timing (morning, afternoon, evening)?

_____

_____

12. What potential distractions should I manage?

_____

_____

13. What rules should I follow concerning hospitality?

_____

_____

14. After the meeting, write down a review of the success of the venue.

What was successful:

_____

_____

What was less successful:

_____

_____

 COACH'S TIP

Use your choice of venue to your advantage

The venue of the negotiation can bring important tactical advantages in itself, especially if you know and take account of your opponent's preferences.

♙♙ COACHING SESSION 37

Being prepared

Answer the following questions to find out how well you are prepared for a forthcoming negotiation.

1. How will you categorize the motives driving your opponent's next negotiation? And how will you know that you are right in this judgement? (For example, are they in expansion or survival mode?)

   _____

   _____

2. How will you categorize their explicit needs? And what opportunities might be provided by implicit needs? (A cost-saving deal may be explicit but ways of achieving it may be implicit, e.g. by cash or staged payments.)

   _____

   _____

3. How do my plans reflect both short- and longer-term goals:

   a) for my organization?

   _____

   _____

   b) for my opponent's organization?

   _____

   _____

4. Who has to give authority in my organization for this potential deal/plan?

   _____

   _____

5. How has that authority been delegated to me?

   _____

   _____

6. How will I establish that my opponents also have delegated authority without demeaning them?

   _____

   _____

7. Which persuasion styles do I prefer to use? Do they work effectively in this sector? (e.g. soft vs hard sell)

_____

_____

8. How might my opponent use 'persuaders' (e.g. social entertainment) way beyond what would be normal in our sector)?

_____

_____

9. If they are unacceptable, how will I refuse without offending?

_____

_____

10. How can I ensure that my negotiation plan appeals to the known interests and preferences of my opponent?

_____

_____

11. Will the place chosen for the meeting be acceptable against ethical criteria?

_____

_____

12. Will it provide all we need for:

a) confidential and meaningful exploration?

_____

_____

b) debate and confirmation?

_____

_____

13. Other things to note:

_____

_____

_____

☐☐ COACHING SESSION 38

Team negotiating

When you are not the only one in the meeting representing your organization, you will need to reflect beforehand on the issues that will arise in such situations.

1. What are the benefits and risks of taking along a 'partner' to a negotiation meeting?

   _____

   _____

   _____

   _____

2. How could we prepare thoroughly, and establish best partnering relations, including the following:

   Who is leading the meeting?

   _____

   Who is recording the meeting?

   _____

   Signals to be used, and for what purpose?

   _____

   Fielding unexpected issues (perhaps requiring consultation and recesses)?

   _____

3. Note any additional points here.

   _____

   _____

   _____

4. How will we establish tactics for handling the following:

   Distractions?_____

   Interruptions?_____

   Disagreements? _____

   Conflict?_____

⏪⏪ COACHING SESSION 39

Developing your skills

Before we go on to examine the practical elements involved in the negotiation meeting, here is your opportunity to rate your skills and targets for improvement. As the environment/climate for negotiation can vary so much from industry (or sector) to industry, there are no right answers about priorities.

1. Think of a negotiator you know and admire, whose scores would be higher than yours (where 1 = low and 9 = highly skilled).
2. Rate yourself for each skill listed in the tables below (where 9 = high priority and 1 = low). Then rate the skills in order of priority and write down your target rating for each one.

Personal skills	Current rating	Priority	Target rating
Plan effectively for negotiation			
Set high aspiration levels			
Think clearly under stress			
Use words well			
Listen, hear and understand well			
Demonstrate integrity			
Exploit power			
Demonstrate open-mindedness			
Demonstrate decisiveness			
Show persistence			

Practical skills	Current rating	Priority	Target rating
Develop win–win objectives			
Control own body language			
Read body language of others			
Sell ideas			
Control discussions			
Summarize/confirm deals			
Negotiate one to one			
Negotiate in a team			
Lead a team negotiation			
Negotiate from the other's perspective			

MAKING A NEGOTIATING PLAN

You should now be able to prepare a negotiation plan, taking into account:

- the motives behind a proposed deal
- explicit and implicit needs arising
- short- and long-term goals (organizational and individual)
- analysis of authority and how decisions are made
- your personal skills and preferences for using persuasion
- the 'opponent' and their preferred venue
- any 'unknowns' that might affect the outcome
- ways to limit any potentially negative influencing power of the environment, conversational tactics, interruptions and crises
- your readiness for the negotiation meeting, after discussions with partners.

ANALYSING BEHAVIOUR

The next part of the case study describes an internal project meeting at BuGS. Read it and apply the behavioural categories for all the interactions (mostly, this means one behaviour per sentence).

Here is a list of behaviours and their initials.

Positive/persuasive:

- Seeking information   (SI)
- Proposing   (Prop)
- Building   (BU)
- Testing understanding   (TU)
- Supporting   (Sup)
- Summarizing   (Sum)
- Reflecting feelings   (R)
- Behaviour labelling   (BL)
- Feelings commentary (exposing/sharing feelings) (FC)

Negative:

- Countering proposals   (CP)
- Shutting out (e.g. over-talking)   (SO)
- Disagreeing   (Dis)

- Blocking   (Bl)
- Defending/attacking   (D/A)
- Irritators (e.g. generous offer)   (Irr)

Neutral:

- Giving information   (GI)

CASE STUDY: BuGS PROJECT MEETING: BEHAVIOUR ANALYSIS

At BuGS an internal meeting is held to decide on priorities for the Computer Implementation Programme. The following people are present:

- Andy, Finance Director (Chair)
- Mac, General Manager, Site No.1
- Terry, Stock Control Manager
- Noel, IT Manager
- Leslie, Buying Director

1. Andy: Welcome everyone – let's make a start, shall we? As you know, the MD has asked me to chair this meeting to work out an agreed timetable for implementing this new financial computer program, which will make our life much easier once it's up and running.

2. Mac: Yeah… when! If it's anything like my past experiences, it'll produce a string of noughts for ages; is it really essential? The sales team needs distractions like this like a 'hole in the head'!

3. Terry: You have my sympathy for that – seems to me that we're in danger of being the fall guys here – and yet we're the ones who make the sales and profits around here! I'm all in favour of a working stock-control system but its implementation could take up months of input time, which we just don't have.

4. Noel: OK! I've heard all that before – rest assured that we'll try to make the changes as painless as possible.

5. Mac (*under his breath*): Heard that before!

6. Andy: Right, we've heard the negatives, but let's put a few facts on the table. The company's paper systems are threatening to strangle our growth. Our suppliers are prepared to commit to an installation programme with their project team doing the hard graft and will see the job through at a pre-agreed contract sum – regardless of how long it takes.

7. Noel: I didn't know that! That's a very good offer – how did you get that?

8. Mac: Was that a result of one of those lunches down at the pub?

9. Andy: No it wasn't! We don't *all* spend all our bonuses there, you know!

10. Leslie: Look, can we get on? I've an important supplier meeting in half an hour and I can't miss it! Andy, have you got a draft timetable to suggest?

11. Andy: Noel – can you pass some copies of the draft schedule around? Start with Leslie!

12. Leslie: I can see straight away that this isn't a consultative meeting at all! Where's the word 'draft' on this paper?

13. Andy: Oh, come on, now – stop looking for trouble – we are trying to agree a schedule that everyone will support – and then we can pass it on to the MD and the Board.

14. Mac: Well, that's something, I suppose – but I want it noted that we don't want any distractions from the sales team on either Mondays or Thursdays! They are our busiest days and sales will suffer if we cannot concentrate our full attention on customers and their deliveries then.

15. Terry: Well said! I'd add in Fridays as well because that's when we do all our re-ordering – and no re-ordering means no stock…

16. Mac: Yeah! And no stock means no sales! QED!

17. Noel: So what you're saying is that we need to concentrate our preparations on Wednesdays, Fridays and weekends?

18. Andy: (*to Noel*) Goodness, will they work at weekends?

19. Noel: I'm sure we can negotiate that!

20. Leslie: Well, that sounds great! Except there'll be an obvious security risk when the security team is away at home. I'm not agreeing to that – it'll be like a free handout!

21. Andy: It sounds to me like we've the basis of an agreement here – I've got to get to a meeting with the bank in a minute. Noel, can you summarize where we've got to and circulate a minute. Do we agree that this can go to the Board Meeting on Friday?

(There is a murmur of support and the meeting breaks up.)

♙♙ COACHING SESSION 40

Assessing the case study: BuGS project meeting

For each entry of the case study, assess the behaviour of the participants against the categories listed above. Make notes for each entry in support of your choice.

Entry	Behaviour category
1	
2	
3	
4	
5	
6	

7	
8	
9	
10	
11	
12	
13	
14	
15	
16	
17	
18	
19	
20	
21	

When you have completed the behaviour assessment, turn to the online resource for our model analysis. Do the same analysis for the case study of the first meeting in Chapter 1.

 ONLINE RESOURCE

Planning checklist

The online resources for this chapter contain a planning checklist you can copy and use as a prompt before each meeting. Go to:

www.TYCoachbooks.com/Negotiation

THE PROD-ProSC MAP

The acronym PROD-ProSC describes the process of a negotiation. This does not mean that yours must follow this pattern but it is a useful way of thinking about all the steps you need to include. The stages are shown in the table below. Your current position on the map is highlighted in bold.

Stage	Issues
P = Prepare	
a) People	What do I know about the culture and style of representatives of this business/organization?
b) Place	**How affected am I likely to be by the personal comfort factors, e.g. distractions, noise and interruptions, seating/layout?**
R = Research	**What is our opponents' position?**
O = Open	How should I open the meeting? What ice-breaking topics might be used? Are there any probing questions I could ask? How could we establish some common ground?
D = Discuss and debate	What style of conversation should I adopt?
Pro = Propose (Conflict management)	How will I resist the temptation to move too quickly/slowly? What if we disagree seriously?
S = Summarize	How good am I at using summaries in meetings?
C = Close	What methods of closing can I use most effectively?

Once you have explored your current stage, note in your action plan any areas that might need more attention.

 NEXT STEPS

You now have the knowledge and skills needed for setting up your meeting, and have identified the factors that can affect the outcome of the discussion.

The next chapter, on opening the meeting, explains how to plan for your opponents' objectives, exploit opportunities for teamwork and weigh up the best ways to isolate and deal with conflict. You will learn how the way you present your case will affect your audience and help you maintain your collaborative position.

👍 TAKEAWAYS

How committed are you to improving your planning and people skills in order to gain improved results? Give some positive examples that illustrate your motivation and determination.

_____

_____

_____

_____

_____

_____

_____

_____

What do you normally do if/when you are challenged with obstructions/objections/hazards?

_____

_____

_____

_____

_____

_____

_____

_____

Given your circumstances, is this the best option? If not, what should you do about it? And who might be able to help?

_____

_____

_____

_____

_____

_____

_____

_____

From the content of this chapter, what else can you do to buttress your objectives and aspirations?

_____

_____

_____

_____

_____

_____

_____

_____

_____

Who do you know (at work or in your social group) who could act as your mentor in buttressing your determination by listening to your experimentations and results (while retaining confidentiality in your business)?

_____

_____

_____

_____

_____

_____

_____

_____

5 | OPENING THE MEETING

 OUTCOMES FROM THIS CHAPTER

- Set the right tone for the meeting and project a positive atmosphere.
- Assess the mood of opponents, identify common ground, preoccupations and objectives.
- Confirm acceptance/formation of the agenda – and the sequence of the discussion.
- Learn about opponents at the meeting through careful 'ice-breaking'.
- Understand how self-presentation approaches can help give your case more impact.
- Assess hidden persuaders and positive behaviours and how to use them successfully.
- Avoid common behaviours that can have a negative effect.

At first sight it may seem superfluous to discuss how to open a meeting, but things said (or not said) in the early stages often set the tone for the rest of the meeting. Carefully managed openings can help negotiators to:

- assess the strength of character and personality of the other person (or team)
- judge their mood and intentions
- understand a little of their background, interests and motivation
- learn about current organizational preoccupations and objectives (and even crises!)
- focus the conversation on a planned agenda – which both parties need to agree.

It might seem unrealistic to expect all negotiations to be held in a relaxed atmosphere – but setting a businesslike tone will help to defuse any latent tensions on either side.

THE NEGOTIATION 'CLIMATE'

Firstly, the psychological climate under which a negotiation is conducted can create a positive or negative atmosphere that can have a marked influence on the ultimate outcome of the negotiation. (We can see, for example, how the climate of a police cell will differ from that of a busy builder's yard.) Effective negotiators pay careful and continuing attention to the negotiation climate – before, during and after each negotiation. Establishment of the right climate is an important component of the overall negotiation strategy.

Three major factors interact to produce the negotiation climate, and the effective negotiator seeks to control each of these:

1. Physical factors

The location and setting for the negotiation can be established to create a particular environment that can have a marked impact on the overall negotiation climate.

2. Temporal factors

There is a 'right time' to commence negotiating, to introduce issues, to use tactics, to make concessions, and for settlement. Appropriate control of time will affect the negotiation climate.

3. Emotional factors

The attitudes and behaviour each negotiator brings to the 'party' affects the opponent and plays a major part in influencing the overall climate.

Through careful manipulation of these three factors, the overall climate suitable to the situation can be controlled.

The factors that can make it easier to persuade others to agree (and/or take action) are frequently discussed and developed in the media. It would be foolish for negotiators to try to imitate their favourite TV hero or media mogul – trying to be someone we clearly are not is an easy way to *reduce* your impact rather than the reverse! However, the following factors can make a positive impact on first impressions. These could make an important difference in a critical meeting (e.g. with opponents who might make subjective or dismissive value judgements).

Here is a reminder of key factors that can have a positive (or negative!) effect on your impact:

Key factor	Examples
Personal presentation	Power dressing, colour coding, grooming
Manner of speech	Power of vocabulary, clarity and correct language
Charm/charisma	The way you are able to present the pleasing side of your personality
Presentation skills	Your ability to speak easily and clearly with people at all levels, to maintain an appropriate pace, and to communicate clearly
Body language	The way you are able to use your own body language to influence your opponent – laid back or 'pushy'

COACHING SESSION 41

Rating your attributes

Rate yourself on the following chart and then ask someone who knows you well to undertake the same task (on a separate piece of paper!) and then compare notes.

Scores:

1 = without positive influence (may even create negative influence)

9 = very influential, positive influence

Attributes	Your perspective (score 1–9)	Colleague's perspective (score 1–9)
Personal presentation		
Manner of speech		
Charm/charisma		
Presentation skills		
Body language		

Ratings here may be subjective – and don't feel disappointed if they are lower than you expected. A practical presentation skills workshop using videoed exercises (with coaching feedback) will reveal some helpful improvement tips (any scores of 5 or less deserve urgent attention in your action plan).

YOUR POWER BASE

Five 'power bases' can be identified within organizations:

1. **Physical** – at its most basic, this means 'I'm bigger/stronger than you are!'

2. **Resource** – 'You have something I want, and I *might* be prepared to share it with you.'

3. **Position** – 'My position gives me power/control over information flow/access to the management system/the right to go about your business.'

4. **Expert** – 'I have expertise in knowledge and skill, which I *may* share with you...'

5. **Personal** – 'I like and trust you – and, together, we appreciate each other's strengths – including our personalities.'

These power bases can be most easily observed in labour-relations negotiations – both internally within trade unions and also in their negotiations with a company or organization's management. The same issues – and outcomes – can be witnessed in commercial and non-commercial organizations – it is just that the application (and sometimes the language) will be different.

COACHING SESSION 42

Analysing your power base

Use this self-analysis chart to help you identify the strength of the two most important job-related factors you use: resource and position. Score yourself using one of the following percentages: 0%, 25%, 50% and 90%. No one has these strengths 100 per cent!

ACCESS TO RESOURCES	How much control over resources do I have for people I negotiate with?
Expertise/advice/knowledge?	
Information?	
Products/services?	
Money or budget?	
Authorizing/commitment of:	
Budgets?	
Cash?	
Expenses?	
Allocation of materials/equipment	
Spares?	
Stationery?	
Communications equipment?	
Tool?	
Time	
Productive time?	
Support time?	
Administration time?	
Staff	
Administrative	
Specialist/technical	

POSITION	How much sharing do I provide?
Access to management policy?	
Current performance standards?	
Forward strategy and plans?	
Needs?	
Access to more senior management?	
Access to specialist support/advisers?	

This analysis will also have demonstrated the degree of trust that has been invested in you by your organization.

WHY NEGOTIATE – OR WHY NOT?

For some people, the thought of 'haggling' is quite intimidating; indeed, many would prefer to remove themselves from any conversation or confrontation that requires any suggestion of a negotiation. That is until they feel that they have been treated unfairly; then, any negotiation may be overtaken by emotions ranging from suspicion, irritation or even anger.

In most customer situations, the free market economy ensures that the customer has a choice – there is always an alternative supplier who desires our business. So, unless we are confronted by a monopolistic situation, it is relatively simple to shrug off any unfortunate supply situation and seek an alternative 'partner', with the thought that 'If you don't want my business, then someone else will!'

Such a reaction does not apply automatically in every situation because:

- the issue at stake is thought to be too small to worry about
- it is thought that there is too little time to set up a new deal with someone else
- the concept of having a preferred client or supplier in the past has proved valuable and protected a partnership – even if this is an informal relationship
- the parties involved actually like (and trust) each other
- both parties prefer to deal with an organization that 'understands us and our needs'.

What can also be heard is the rejection of a negotiation offer when there is a resistance to apply a flexible approach: 'If you cannot afford our products/services, you are in the wrong market/shop/store!'

These two stances may feel destructive – and without some movement or change, they will certainly not lead to a win/win deal – and any debate is likely to be a waste of time, or lose/lose.

However, don't be misled by lose/lose stories you may have heard about in the press. Lose/lose outcomes may make interesting reading in newspapers – and help their sales – but, otherwise, they probably only lead to misunderstandings about the negotiating process. Don't be fooled into believing that most negotiations have only a win/lose or lose/lose outcome.

GREETINGS WITH PERSONALITY

A typical business greeting (in the West) involves a handshake and this can transmit quite a lot of information about the social skills and personality of the individual. Handshakes can range from the 'power-crazed-crusher' to the 'wet-fish'. Much has been read into these extremes (not to mention the additional factors of whose hand is in the dominant position – or what it might mean when the other 'controlling' person also clasps your elbow with their spare hand), but certainly these factors have an effect on other people, and may also tell us something about the other person's awareness of this. (Negotiators who are working internationally should obtain detailed advice on different forms of greeting – and other behaviours – that may apply in their chosen cultures.)

With virtual meetings – over the telephone or in electronic exchanges – the rules about conveying the right impression are the same but the application is obviously different. A smile in the voice and persuasive use of vocabulary can work wonders – but can be difficult to maintain if a session of cold-calling has brought persistent brush-offs. And emails can easily convey the wrong tone, and come across as dictatorial or impolite.

The truth is that the lack of visual feedback can make remote contact very tricky when the other party is not already a real prospect for your product or service or has some pressing need requiring a solution.

COACH'S TIP

Make your prospect warm to you

While the absence of good manners may tell us a great deal about another person, it does not always make the individual any better or worse as a negotiator – or more or less trustworthy. (For further consideration of these aspects, you could do little better than to read Dale Carnegie's classic book *How to Win Friends and Influence People*.) However, on the whole, people don't make agreements if they are unhappy with the greeting or treatment they have received.

ONLINE RESOURCE

Understanding behaviour and ego states

The online resources for this chapter provide valuable information about how to look out for and manage people who behave strangely and might disrupt your attempts to negotiate a serious deal. We need to remember that, as all people are individuals, unusual behaviour in meetings that involve interpersonal skills can occur but that there are simple ways of managing such situations and still achieve a positive result. Go to:

www.TYCoachbooks.com/Negotiation

EGO STATES

You will have read that mature people ought to converse with one another as adults – sensible, serious, factual and, mostly, engaging with others in a thoughtful frame of mind. However, our environment and the people around us can affect our response considerably. You may have an adult friend whose lifestyle and conversational mood is closer to the behaviour of a much younger person, or even a child. He or she is light-hearted, full of fun and quite excitable. Such people are good fun to be with when you are off-duty on a night out. This description could also fit an enthusiastic salesperson with an impressive sales record.

At the other end of the scale, you might also have met serious-minded people who look at life from the perspective of a parent – either critical and disciplining or supportive and caring. Ideally, your interactions in a negotiation need to achieve the same aim – you are two adults negotiating factually and arriving at a deal that you both believe is balanced, fair and capable of implementation. All this sounds a great deal easier than it often is in real life. (An online resource will extend this discussion for those who wish to explore the subject in more depth.)

The challenge that arises comes from circumstances (or motives) beyond our control – and possibly beyond that of our opponent as well. The result can be that the last state of mind he or she may adopt is that of a rational, clear-thinking adult who will appreciate a reasoned case!

THE MEANING OF MOODS

The moment you enter a host's office, you should try to assess the mood of your opponent, which can give a fair indication of how negotiations may progress. Highly skilled influencers see these early stages as good opportunities to establish a positive footing for the meeting from the start. This may be through careful 'pacing' of the other person's speech patterns and mirroring their body language. Some measure of old-fashioned charm may also help the meeting along. Even so, the other party may give off strong, negative or cold feelings and it is easy to assume that these are directed solely at you or your organization.

But this may not be the case: for example, the person you are meeting may have had a simply dreadful morning – fallen over the cat on their way downstairs, crashed the car on their way down to the railway station, missed their train, and then discovered that the departmental budget has been sliced in half without any consultation. After such a series of negative events, anyone could be excused for being a little icy.

So, if you are visiting with the intention of re-establishing a service contract that has lapsed (and resulted in some rather high and unexpected bills for your client), you may well assume the worst (that the cold atmosphere is solely directed at you) and that you are on a loser from the start. This is understandable – but wrong! The organization still needs to continue with the service your organization provides and would benefit from the revised contract that you may be able to offer.

COACH'S TIP

Don't take mood personally

Remember that some negotiators use harsh tactics to unsettle their opponent at the start of a meeting – and, if you suspect this tactic, you need to have a strategy for handling the situation. A thick skin and plenty of patience will help.

HANDLING EMOTIONAL SITUATIONS

When negotiators have worked together for a long period (say, a year or more), they will have a level of understanding and appreciation of each other's personality and outlook on life and business. So if, after a normal telephone call from your opponent to set up a meeting, you find them in an emotional state when you arrive (head in hands, office in a mess, and not offering any of the usual greetings or eye contact), it can come as something of a shock.

The alarm bells should be ringing: could the reason for this demanded, 'unusual' meeting originate in your organization? If so, the apologies may already be forming in your mind. With the benefit of a secure environment/meeting room it may be possible to provide a listening ear and help your opponent to feel that, whatever the problem, it is not the end of the world. (This could be a case where your listening ear – or 'caring parent' – may be able to help your opponent feel less like a depressed child and recover as a mature adult.) You need to achieve this before effective negotiation is likely to be possible. In terms of priorities, this conversation may have little to do with your objectives – but will this person be in the mood to transact business while trying to take in and deal with problems?

Counselling techniques could be useful in such a situation, and could lead to disclosure of relationship problems that your contact has never previously revealed – maybe with his/her boss, deputy, or even family. You may reel from this idea of playing nursemaid to someone in the working environment but, clearly, in these circumstances your business meeting will not progress satisfactorily and your support for your client or supplier could help them commit to you in the long term – and defeat any impression that selfish negotiators are interested only in achieving their objectives.

ᏗᏗ COACHING SESSION 43

Restoring emotional balance

Think about your business contacts (both internal and external) and project the kinds of difficulties each person might be facing, given your understanding of their situations. (Take care that this confidential document cannot be read by 'unauthorized people' and maybe 'code' any references to specific personnel – just in case!)

_____

_____

_____

_____

_____

_____

_____

_____

_____

_____

! COACH'S TIP

Help your colleague

Your first golden rule should always be to try to help stabilize your contact with the aim of restoring their 'balance' so that an objective discussion and agreement can be achieved, even if the outcome is a revised appointment date.

HOW IS YOUR INFLUENCE?

When we have influence, we become so used to its effect that we are tempted to believe that it will be permanent. However, this is rarely true. For example, the power to coerce people depends on their compliance and, if that breaks down, so does the power of the influence.

Compliance can work against the influencer – as the person on the receiving end may accept the influence only as a way to get the influencer to do what he or she wants. An example of this might have been selling a product at the supplier's determined price so that the supplier continues to supply the product or service – even though, in private, you might disagree with the principle. In the UK this principle of price fixing, or resale price maintenance, is illegal.

However, if a person identifies with another and attempts to be like that person in image, behaviour or beliefs, this may be flattering but may occur only in private. In other words, the apparent influence is only temporary. If the influence is internalized (which tends to occur when the influencing behaviour matches that person's internal beliefs), the change becomes incorporated into the person's internal value system and will therefore be long-lasting.

COACHING SESSION 44

Assessing your influence

Identify some occasions when you felt you had influence.

1. When was your influence permanent?

2. When was it temporary?

3. When was it a failure?

EXPLORING PERSONAL BACKGROUND

Many mistakes have been made in meetings through negotiators rushing into a business discussion without exploring the possible common ground they share with their opponent. (The Japanese have much to teach us in this field.) Since a service contract may last, initially, for two or three years or even longer, it is very important to build good relationships and to have a clear understanding of the other party. This might well extend to consideration of professional background, family life, hobbies and career aims – and, especially, gaining insights into the other person's culture, values and integrity. In other words, the parties are piecing together a full picture of their opponent's background and the degree to which they might be trusted in a partnering kind of relationship.

COACH'S TIP

Find common ground

Common ground can be exceptionally valuable when external events conspire to divide you and your organizations.

EXPLORING THE BUSINESS BACKGROUND

General discussion at the start of a meeting gives the participants the opportunity to explore current aims, success stories and the possible challenges being experienced in business life. This 'tuning-in' process can be extremely valuable as genuine information may be revealed about their business that could be of great interest in subsequent discussions of the business agenda. This phase also provides negotiators with the opportunity to set the scene with information about their organization's needs or philosophy and preoccupations. The key point to remember here is that all the players in a negotiation should be able to 'sell' their organization's needs and objectives. Good selling skills should not be seen as the sole province of the salesperson.

COACHING SESSION 45

Moving on

Have you ever felt that a meeting was making too little progress – but that your assessment did not seem to be shared by others in the room? It could be that your partners do share your irritation but that they, too, are unsure what to do about it. Such incidents could indicate that our opponents are uncertain that the timing is right to commit to a deal – and are therefore filling in time!

How would you feel about the following situations and what steps would you take?

1. Conversation that seems to be filling time

   Feelings: _____

   _____

   Actions: _____

   _____

2. Reluctance to commit to a precise position

   Feelings: _____

   _____

   Actions: _____

   _____

3. Inability to distinguish what can be negotiated from things that cannot be changed

   Feelings: _____

   _____

   Actions: _____

   _____

4. 'Fogging' – too many words used to describe plain and simple concepts

   Feelings: _____

   _____

   Actions: _____

   _____

5. Repetition of 'speeches' that intend to inform/educate/teach rather than gain movement/agreement/commitment

   Feelings: _____

   _____

   Actions: _____

   _____

COACH'S TIP

Judge your opponent's mood

Take into account your opponent's mood, which could have a distinct effect on reaching a satisfactory outcome for your meeting. Existing partners should not present a challenge, but new contacts may bring both uncertainty and possible risks (of misjudgement or inappropriate comments) that could jeopardize a deal.

INTRODUCING THE AGENDA

Clearly, any business meeting should have an agenda if a measurable outcome is to be achieved. The agenda should, preferably, have been set in advance of the meeting. Even a meeting set up to work out new business will benefit from an agenda, if only to establish specific goals and the timescale needed for them to be achieved. All this assumes that both parties have agreed to the items on the agenda and are committed to cover the brief that the agenda sets.

If the meeting is called to resolve a complaint or disagreement, time might need to be less prescribed, but some checklist of items is still likely to be needed if the discussion is to lead to an agreed outcome. After the introductions, the parties at the meeting need to confirm the items on the agenda – and should ensure that any feelings about them are signalled before jumping into the deep end of any potential conflict. This should enable both parties to cope with any difficulties and prevent a surprise attack.

COACH'S TIP

Respect dress codes

For many decades the City of London worked on the principle that the 'uniform' of a pinstriped suit conveyed a traditional culture – and this had the effect of making negotiators feel comfortable with one another. Such standards may be puzzling if you have not experienced the dress codes used in a closed industry but, when new deals are being struck between vendors and clients who have not met before, appearance can be important. Failure to pay attention to the expectations of the other party can result in the loss of an important deal.

👥 COACHING SESSION 46

Underhand tactics

Consider the following scenario. Two young female sales consultants are discussing the week's appointments in a hotel lobby. On discovering that her first call the next day has previously been visited by her colleague, the first representative is heard to ask: 'Is he [the client] the type of man who would appreciate a light-hearted, flirtatious manner or would you recommend more formality?'

However much such plans and tactics might be deprecated, it has to be remembered that some of your opponents may be influenced by them.

If these people were in your team, how might you interpret this conversation and what advice would you give them, bearing in mind your knowledge of ego states, described earlier in this chapter?

_____

_____

_____

_____

_____

_____

BULLYING TACTICS

Nikita Khrushchev, one-time diminutive leader of the USSR during the height of the Cold War, sent shock waves around the world with his unrestrained response to a debate at the United Nations. Interrupting a particularly significant discussion, he removed one of his shoes and banged it aggressively on the table before him as he shouted 'Niet!' ('No!')

Dom Mintoff, Prime Minister of Malta, perpetrated similar dramatic effects in his negotiations with the British over the future of the Royal Naval base there. He was known to lose his temper when a meeting did not go his way, stand on his chair and shake his fist at his opponents – using the full psychological advantage of the extra height.

Bullying of this kind can be effective in negotiating meetings – especially where the opponent has little alternative but to deal with the person doing the bullying. However, while use – or misuse – of power can be very effective in the short term, it can generate determined opposition in the longer term.

COACHING SESSION 47

Dealing with drama

Consider whether you have ever witnessed anger, bullying or bad temper or another dramatic situation in a meeting.

1. How did you or a colleague handle it?

   _____

   _____

   _____

2. Was it dealt with successfully? If so, why, and if not, why not?

   _____

   _____

   _____

3. How would you handle a similar situation in the future?

   _____

   _____

   _____

Within the constraints of hierarchy, it is generally best to field the most persuasive negotiator – especially when the client or opponent has known preferences. This advice might not match our ideas for an equal and egalitarian society but negotiators should not confuse their agenda objectives in such meetings.

COACHING SESSION 48

Hiding your emotions

Answer the following questions about your level of self-control.

1. How able are you to hide your disapproval of bad manners or other inappropriate behaviour?

   _____

   _____

   _____

2. How able are you to control your feelings when something funny happens?

_____

_____

_____

3. How would you react to an unexpected complaint against your organization?

_____

_____

_____

THE SALES PERSPECTIVE

Failure to pay attention to the expectations of the other party can result in the loss of an important deal. (And this could extend into the future.) Expectations of salespeople are very wide and generalized. The role of the salesperson may be obvious but understanding of it is often oversimplified. The saying 'Nothing can be bought if it has not first been sold' is a pithy description of the salesperson's position but the odds can, on occasion, seem to be loaded against the salesperson when the negotiating power appears to lie with the buyer (who controls the budget). Is it surprising that salespeople are sometimes thought of as being superficial and/or 'economical with the truth' in pursuit of a sale?

Actually, the sales role can be extremely satisfying, especially when targets are being met and buyers value the advice and intelligence that is on offer. The role provides:

- a ready sense of achievement when targets are met
- recognition and appreciation of the salesperson's technical advice
- day-by-day variety from a role that mixes people, prospects and places
- a sense of responsibility as the role has a major influence on the success of a company.

However, the role can be full of frustration if a salesperson feels undervalued by clients and if any other of the above 'satisfiers' are missing. Still worse is if they are 'attacked' by successive buyers; this will lead to strong negative feelings about the role – hardly the best starting position for any negotiation.

Naive salespeople may assume that:

- buyers hold all the cards and they know what they want/need
- price is the only bargaining counter

- the competition has better products/services/prices
- price cutting is the best motivator for a sale.

THE BUYER'S NEEDS

Buyers have needs as well – and astute sales professionals will seek to satisfy as many of them as possible. They include the need to:

- have their voice heard
- avoid risk and 'trouble'
- be thought of as 'fair and nice'
- make difficult decisions (possibly with help)
- avoid learning about suppliers' operations second-hand
- gain support at times of trouble
- receive a good explanation (especially when things go wrong!)
- look good within their organization.

RECOGNIZING COMMON INTERESTS

If the relationship between negotiators is to thrive and grow to maturity – as might be wished – it would not be unusual for interests in common to be discovered. This is not proposed as a vital aim (which could impose an unreasonable objective) but simply illustrates that a first supply contract *could* then realistically progress to a five-year plan – bringing almost a partnering role between trusted business associates. This kind of relationship is demonstrable – even today, when so many sectors have had to meet intense, inward competition. As we have seen, the real basis of a lasting relationship is goodwill – based on repeat business contracts.

This kind of partnering can lead to the following benefits:

- Increased business/volume
- Extensions to existing contracts
- A broader range of agreements (e.g. product or services)
- Improved terms
- Referrals for new potential business
- Adjustments to product/service specifications to suit client needs

COACHING SESSION 49

Partnering

Consider the following questions as they apply to your current role.

1. What examples of partnering can you give that have enabled you to meet your objectives – broadly meeting the descriptions above? List three examples here.

   a) _____

   b) _____

   c) _____

2. Consider what evaluation might be applied to these examples by your partner(s); would they consider the examples as successful for them? If not, why not?

   a) _____

   b) _____

   c) _____

3. What steps will you take now to develop strategic partnerships from your negotiating relationships? (Add these to your personal action plan.)

   a) _____

   b) _____

   c) _____

COACH'S TIP

Value partnering

Partnering can help negotiators maintain their position at the top of their market. No deal is impervious to being challenged by a competitor and there is always the risk of losing future business to new, aggressive entrants. Partnering helps protect against this.

◊◊ COACHING SESSION 50

Hidden persuaders: help for partnering

The purpose of this questionnaire is for you to highlight behaviours and habits in your negotiating partners that may have an impact on your negotiating success. Rate your partners by placing a circle around the appropriate score (where 1 = rarely and 6 = often) according to how you think they typically react in encounters with opponents. Compare this with your own behaviours from coaching session 34 and see how you differ. Where you identify the areas where they are rather better – or weaker – than you are, you can use this information to plan accordingly.

This is a person who...	Rating
1 Likes to listen to other people talk	1 2 3 4 5 6
2 Encourages others to talk	1 2 3 4 5 6
3 Listens equally well to: friends acquaintances family	1 2 3 4 5 6 1 2 3 4 5 6 1 2 3 4 5 6
4 Behaves in an uninhibited way in all situations	1 2 3 4 5 6
5 Copies other people's behaviour in meetings	1 2 3 4 5 6
6 Resists other people's attempts to influence them	1 2 3 4 5 6
7 Controls their own non-verbal behaviour	1 2 3 4 5 6
8 Observes other people's behaviour	1 2 3 4 5 6
9 Talks through one/both hands in front of their mouth	1 2 3 4 5 6
10 Uses a firm handshake on meeting	1 2 3 4 5 6
11 Maintains strong eye contact during conversations	1 2 3 4 5 6
12 Uses a relaxed/laid-back posture	1 2 3 4 5 6
13 Leaves off tasks/reading to talk or listen to others	1 2 3 4 5 6
14 Looks at the speaker	1 2 3 4 5 6
15 Ignores distractions while talking/listening	1 2 3 4 5 6
16 Smiles/nods/encourages the speaker to talk	1 2 3 4 5 6
17 Thinks about what is said	1 2 3 4 5 6
18 Uses hand/arm gestures during speech	1 2 3 4 5 6
19 Plays with a pen/calculator, etc. during a conversation	1 2 3 4 5 6
20 Folds arms when listening	1 2 3 4 5 6
21 Discloses emotions readily through facial expressions	1 2 3 4 5 6
22 Observes facial feedback/reaction to your talk	1 2 3 4 5 6
23 Imitates the other person's posture	1 2 3 4 5 6
24 Controls uninhibited behaviour in conversation	1 2 3 4 5 6
25 Tries to understand the speaker's meaning	1 2 3 4 5 6

26 Tries to understand *why* the speaker is communicating	1 2 3 4 5 6
27 Lets the speaker finish what he/she is saying	1 2 3 4 5 6
28 Encourages the speaker to finish if he/she hesitates	1 2 3 4 5 6
29 Restates what is said to check understanding	1 2 3 4 5 6
30 Experiences uncertainty in speech (ums and ers)	1 2 3 4 5 6
31 Uses silence in conversations	1 2 3 4 5 6
32 Is insulated against the irritators/fidgeting of speakers	1 2 3 4 5 6
33 Observes the other's willingness to hear out a long speech by watching their eye gaze	1 2 3 4 5 6
34 Moves away/closer when listening	1 2 3 4 5 6
35 Runs hand through hair while talking	1 2 3 4 5 6
36 Rubs palms together when listening/speaking	1 2 3 4 5 6
37 Withholds judgement until a speaker has finished	1 2 3 4 5 6
38 Listens to ideas – not the manner or choice of words	1 2 3 4 5 6
39 Listens, even though the next words/ideas can be anticipated	1 2 3 4 5 6
40 Asks the speaker to define/explain technical/unfamiliar words	1 2 3 4 5 6

A marking guide is contained in the online resources. Check your ratings against those given there and think about how you might tactfully engage your negotiating partners in managing their 'hidden persuaders' more effectively. Go to:
www.TYCoachbooks.com/Negotiation

 COACH'S TIP

Work on your action points

Action points need to be prioritized – working on three or four points every couple of months – with a trusted colleague (or even a friend who is *not* involved in your business). After achieving some progress, move on to another four improvement areas. Using video coaching, where you can record and play back your performance and analyse it, will help a great deal.

Agreeing on agenda items

Setting out your agenda for a meeting and sharing (or, better still, exchanging) it with your opponent, helps both parties confirm preparations on their case and enables logical discussion and a possible agreement to be reached. It will also help to reduce any feelings of uncertainty and suspicion that can make reaching an agreement difficult. A list of needs or goals is essential – and finding relationships between agenda items will help progress the meeting. However, it is not a good plan to prepare a fixed, sequential approach: flexibility will enable opponents' objectives to be tied together into an overall agreement.

BEHAVIOUR AND ATTITUDES

In any negotiation, the following behaviours and attitudes are prevalent. Some have positive and some negative effects, and these can be broken down into nine basic categories.

Negative behaviours include:

1. **Irritants:** certain words in common use that can have a negative effect on the opposition

2. **Counter-proposals:** trying to 'score' by opposing suggestions

3. **Defence and attack spirals:** conflict without reason

4. **Argument dilution:** trying for the lowest common denominator of a series of arguments advanced to support a negotiating position.

Positive behaviours include:

5. **Behaviour labelling**: indicating a class of behaviour that is about to be used

6. **Testing understanding and summarizing:** consolidation of how the negotiation is going

7. **Reflection:** usually a repeat of a statement in the form of a question

8. **Information seeking:** questioning to gain the necessary information to carry on with the negotiation

9. **Feelings commentary:** letting the opposition know how you feel.

COACHING SESSION 51

Analysing the effects of behaviour and attitudes

1. Of the nine behaviours and attitudes listed above, which have you experienced or witnessed?

   _____

2. Which do you use?

   _____

3. What effects did they have on you and the meeting? Think about the effects that the negative behaviours had on your wish to continue with the interaction. Contrast this with the more positive reactions that the positive behaviours brought out.

_____

_____

_____

_____

4. Negative behaviours that you will try to avoid in future:

_____

_____

_____

_____

5. Positive behaviours that you will practise using to gain more influence:

_____

_____

_____

This chapter has set out a formal structure for negotiations, which should help ensure that even the less experienced negotiator will be able to avoid some common errors. Sometimes, short cuts can achieve good results but the reverse outcome is always a possibility, so this formal approach provides a valuable 'safety net'.

Carefully managed openings help negotiators to:

- assess the characters and personalities of the other team
- judge the mood of the others attending
- understand a little of their background, interests and motivation
- learn about current organizational preoccupations, objectives and even crises.

THE PRO-ProSC MAP

The stages of the PROD-ProSC process are shown in the table below. Your current position on the map is highlighted in bold.

Stage	Issues
P = Prepare a) People b) Place	What do I know about the culture and style of representatives of this business/organization? How affected am I likely to be by the personal comfort factors, e.g. distractions, noise and interruptions, seating/layout?
R = Research	What is our opponents' position?
O = Open	**How should I open the meeting?** **What ice-breaking topics might be used?** **Are there any probing questions I could ask?** **How could we establish some common ground?**
D = Discuss and debate	What style of conversation should I adopt?
Pro = Propose Conflict management	How will I resist the temptation to move too quickly/slowly? What if we disagree seriously?
S = Summarize	How good am I at using summaries in meetings?
C = Close	What methods of closing can I use most effectively?

Once you have explored your current stage, note in your action plan any areas that might need more attention.

NEXT STEPS

This chapter on opening a negotiation meeting has outlined various factors to consider so that you can get the meeting off to a good start.

In the next chapter you will learn how to control the debate and progress your objectives through open discussion within the structure of your meeting, using assertive behaviour and avoiding emotional distractions.

👍 TAKEAWAYS

What is your plan to set the right tone for the meeting and project a positive atmosphere?

_____

_____

_____

_____

_____

_____

How have you assessed the mood of your opponents, identified common ground, preoccupations and objectives?

_____

_____

_____

_____

_____

_____

How have you agreed and confirmed acceptance of the agenda and sequence of discussion?

_____

_____

_____

_____

_____

_____

How will you learn more about your opponents at the meeting?

_____

_____

_____

_____

_____

What aspects of your presentation will give your case more impact?

_____

_____

_____

_____

_____

How will you assess and use hidden persuaders and positive behaviours?

_____

_____

_____

_____

_____

How will you avoid common behaviours that can have a negative effect?

_____

_____

_____

_____

_____

6 | CONTROLLING THE DEBATE

 OUTCOMES FROM THIS CHAPTER

- Recognize the value of information exchange through open discussion.

- Progress your negotiation objectives.

- Use assertive behaviour by resisting the temptations of an emotional climate.

- Control conversation through the power of listening so that emotional distractions are avoided/controlled.

- Maintain a meeting structure to avoid confusion.

- Practise the use of assertive behaviour.

Entering any negotiation assumes that the parties are prepared to change their minds – or at least modify them. This principle underpins the whole purpose of a discussion. Two parties can have a disagreement or dispute but a successful deal is only likely to be achieved when both parties are able to sit down and rationally talk through their differences with the ultimate motive of trading amicably or agreeing on a process to resolve the issues logically and calmly.

All this sounds easy – but real life involves people who have been hurt, feel cheated or are suspicious, or even determined to maintain the upper hand and rub their opponents' noses in the dirt! So, debating an issue (or a series of them) requires all sides to be prepared to move away from past (now opening) positions so that a new agreement can be forged. In the most intractable cases, such a movement could take weeks, months and even years – a process which requires the build-up of trust through much open but rational debate (as one-time UK Prime Minister, Sir Harold Macmillan, said, 'Jaw-Jaw is better than War-War').

Emotions may be raw and not fully resolved unless, and until, they are voiced. Luckily, in commerce and industry, disputes are generally resolved rather more speedily – and those that are not may be progressed through the involvement of mediators, legal advisers and, possibly, legal action (with the risk of negative publicity). Mostly, the power of debate brings the chance of rational people seeing beyond emotional issues to arrive at agreement through compromise: the feeling that both sides achieve a win/win.

THE IMPORTANCE OF VALUES

Issues that are fundamental to healthy relationships between people at work include the value of:

- respecting one another as human beings
- politeness and good manners
- valuing others' knowledge, experience and ideas
- wishing to build win/win relationships and deals
- gaining support for your plans and initiatives
- celebrating success over a period of time.

This is not to say that all negotiations *must* lead to long-lasting collaborative relationships. There will be occasions when deals must be achieved that have decidedly short-term aims – with little expectation of any enduring outcomes. That is acceptable. What is undesirable is leading your opponents to believe claims that are misleading, for example that business will be long term (in order to gain special rates) when this is not the case. However, information is generally free at the point of delivery – and negotiation often depends upon insightful information.

STYLE VERSUS SUBSTANCE

We are probably all experienced attenders at meetings, in both social and business settings. Many meetings will have little purpose other than to achieve an update of recent activities and results – or even just to gain an insight into people's morale and health. When internal meetings are held and it has not been thought essential to issue an agenda, the discussion may wander around and be driven by whoever has the most interesting topics to share. There is a place for such updates – and, surprisingly, quite a lot of commercial calls made are of this type – by representatives calling on their clients at seasonal times or buyers dropping into their showrooms when it is convenient to a buying trip.

In the employee relations sector, such opportunities are valuable for sharing worries or difficulties; sometimes a quick word indicating unhappiness about a situation can stimulate a discreet investigation and some action on a minor problem that avoids a major issue arising. However, if negotiations are likely to be involved, every negotiator should prepare thoroughly before entering into a more formal discussion, or the results could be very embarrassing.

COACH'S TIP

Prepare and agree on key points

An agenda should be prepared and agreed, even if there is just one item on it. It does not have to be a formal agenda – an email will achieve the same purpose – but clarity is advisable before the meeting is set up. This will help avoid the meeting descending into argument about different issues that the convenor of the meeting did not expect or plan for. This is all part of making sure that confusion is avoided during every step of the process – and that all parties are clear about what is to happen.

LOGIC VERSUS 'SPAGHETTI'

At its simplest level, the process of discussing key points on an agenda involves reaching agreement on the method to be adopted. This sounds easy, especially when negotiators are used to debating topics in a sequential way – i.e. agreement on point A should lead to discussion on point B, and so on – but this assumes agreement over a certain way of working, and some people (and different cultures) may want to work in a much less formal way.

Less easy is a debate that involves one overall, complex topic that threatens to 'lurk in a bowl' (rather like spaghetti) – and, no matter how hard the negotiators try, the ends seem determined to hide – making it impossible for the parties to agree topics, a sequence and therefore any lasting agreement. This would be hard enough when both negotiators are 'disabled' in such a discussion – but much more frustrating is when just one person seems determined to confuse by avoiding any logical sequence for debate and constantly moves the ground, changing topics with terms such as: '...And another thing' or 'Pity your company didn't think about that when increasing prices without warning last year!'

Such tactics can be exasperating (could that be their intention?) and the opponent has little option but to try, calmly, to absorb the frustration and lead the opponent back to agenda topics. (This is vital – or nothing will ever be achieved.) To be successful here, the rational negotiator needs unlimited patience and determination (coupled with the ability to exhaust built-up frustration on the squash court or in a swimming pool).

COACH'S TIP

Ignore one-upmanship

It is better to ignore competitive tactics than attempt to join in with them. If you retaliate, it will simply become a time-wasting 'competition' with no winners. Your reputation as a sensible person will be damaged.

COACHING SESSION 52

Discussion tactics

There are nine strategies and tactics commonly used by negotiators and influencers. Which of them can you identify from your field of work or life? And which have you used?

1. Informational: this refers to what is actually contained in the communication and not to any attribute of the influencer.

Are *you* a 'detail' person? Who do you know who uses this style? And how successful are they?

_____

_____

How could you use this style and gain greater success?

_____

_____

_____

(NB: Overuse of this style could cause confusion and give opponents 'earache'!)

2. Coercive: this is based on the ability of the influencer to punish, force or compel.

Who do you know who uses this style? Does it work and, if so, why?

_____

_____

Are *you* a coercive person? What could be the results of working this way?

_____

_____

_____

(NB: there is a risk that coercive behaviour can result in placid acceptance rather than creative enthusiasm for implementation.)

3. Reward: this is based on the ability of the influencer to manipulate rewards, e.g. commission, profit margins, bonuses, order quantities.

Do *you* emphasize reward in your persuasion/negotiation meetings? What are the results?

_____

_____

Who do you know who uses this style? What are the advantages and disadvantages?

How could you make it work in your situation – without setting a precedent?

4. Referent: this stems from the influenced person liking or identifying with the influencer.

Do *you* consciously encourage people to like you? What difference does it make in your negotiations with them?

How do *you* feel when they are less influenced than you would prefer? And how might this change your relationship afterwards?

5. Expert: this is the attribution of superior knowledge or ability to the influencer by the influenced.

Who do you know who exploits this style? What effects does it have?

How does it influence the relationship between you?

(NB: Don't overwhelm others with your expertise; if you do, you may find that opponents want to wait until you are on holiday to engage in future negotiations!)

6. Legitimate: this is based on general norms (e.g. custom and practice) about what is appropriate behaviour in your/their sector (i.e. business, charity, voluntary body).

Who around you consciously uses their authority or job status to influence others? How successfully does it work?

7. Compliance: this is where a person accepts influence as a way to get the other person to do what is wanted.

Put another way, does anyone have a hold over you? How did this loss of independence arise?

_____

_____

Have *you* ever used this approach with someone else? What could be the long-term effects?

_____

_____

8. Identification: one person identifies with another and attempts to be like the other person. (The film *Single White Female* illustrates this situation perfectly.)

Have you noticed anyone trying to 'steal' your identity and remove your independence of thought? What was the result?

_____

_____

If not, might it ever apply in *your* situation? What would be the risks and how could you disentangle yourself?

_____

_____

Have you ever identified with someone close to you – and how did the other person respond?

_____

_____

9. Internalization: influence is accepted because the tactics show similarities with the other party's system of values and are therefore acceptable to them.

Has this method ever compromised *your* position, to the point that you no longer notice it? (This could apply to use of language, attitudes, performance or lifestyle, etc.)

_____

_____

Some of the above strategies may seem entirely fanciful – but, with careful reflection, you will recognize some of them and you may then find yourself wondering how some decisions in your environment were made and whether undue influence could have been at work. Would that be wrong? As long as no dishonesty is involved, this kind of influence is probably not unethical; it depends on your attitude to the saying: 'There is no such thing as a free lunch.'

It remains the role of your organization to spell out clear policies on what is legitimate and ethical. Your own attitude towards these matters will guide you. (Press investigations frequently point to scandals caused through someone failing to follow appropriate 'principles'. Is it sufficient to worry only about ensuring that you are not caught? Questionable behaviour in negotiating means that at least one other person (or organization) is aware of what has happened. Could they use that knowledge against you in some future situation?)

COMPETITION VERSUS CO-OPERATION

It is some people's nature to be competitive in almost everything (watch people queuing for a plane, especially those without allocated seats). For some, the opportunity to win an argument with a senior manager, assert their superiority over colleagues or forcefully make their point is just too tempting to resist – and we all know how irritating that can be. No matter where these tactics originate, it is best to ignore them and move on. It might be tempting to join in such 'wind-ups' but there is an expectation that managers will behave more like adults (or even parents) than children.

Co-operation and collaboration are the tactics most likely to lead to win/win outcomes in negotiation.

 ONLINE RESOURCE

Co-operative tactics

For more on this topic, and for the model answer to Coaching session 53, go to:

www.TYCoachbooks.com/Negotiating

COACHING SESSION 53

Co-operative negotiation

Here are some characteristics of co-operative bargaining. Rate yourself on the following scale:

1 = Scarcely applies to me

2 = Mostly applies

3 = Applies all the time.

Co-operative characteristic	1	2	3
A. Happy to interact with opponents			
B. Interested in their needs			
C. Willing to share information, open and trusting			
D. Rational and using little emotion			
E. Regard parties as collaborators (rather than adversaries)			
F. Start with more reasonable/realistic demands			
G. Flexible (usually having authority to work this way)			
H. Ask questions rather than make statements			
I. Reciprocate in making concessions			
J. Discuss compromise, rather than using power to coerce			
K. Seek solution from mutual problem-solving			
L. Look for a win/win outcome (or no losers)			

Find out what your scores mean in the online resources for this chapter.

SOCIAL AND POLITICAL PRESSURES

In Chapter 5 we explored strategies used by negotiators working in the sales and procurement sectors. We saw that both specialisms can exhibit extrovert behaviour but that when persuasive goals are achieved they can cement good relationships between negotiators from opposing sides (e.g. marketing and purchasing). Such 'partnering' is an excellent example of how win/win relationships can develop when joint business has been successfully conducted for a number of years.

Unfortunately, such collaborative behaviour is not always so obvious in negotiations in the employee relations sector, which has often been marked by disputes, name-calling and expensive disruptions. Sadly, rational discussion can fall prey to provocative outbursts, epitomized by:

- 'blow and counter-blow'

- accusations

- emotional exaggeration

- anger and reprisals

- grandstanding.

Achieving positive results through a calm exchange of views sounds easy – but emotional outbursts may lead to a form of 'gamesmanship' where rational argument can lose out to dramatic effects. This can result from:

- exaggeration

- extreme political argument

- use of emotional case histories

- a desire to win every argument.

It is often argued that extreme behaviour in this 'amphitheatre' is simply about gaining everyone's attention so that the case is not brushed aside and ignored, but the big risk is that the 'audience' is sufficiently irritated that they go 'deaf' and become determined to refuse the case.

COACHING SESSION 54

Reputations and disputes

The following checklist provides a positive reminder of some key issues. Tick those that you are already doing and put a cross against any that you have not prepared for and could be a threat to your success.

1. Preparation

   1. Have we clear objectives for the case? (LFP > MFP; see Chapter 3) ☐

   2. Are we prepared to move from our starting position? ☐

   3. Do we have a timescale for settlement? ☐

   4. Have we prepared a strategy for obtaining movement? ☐

   5. Do we have an adjournment strategy? ☐

2. Maintaining and building trust

   6. Ensuring that opponents do not lose credibility in front of their team ☐

   7. Not withdrawing an unconditional offer once it is made ☐

   8. Not appealing to the opposition directly until after negotiation ☐

   9. Ensuring no 'trickery' in the final agreement ☐

   10. Ensuring that the final bargain is implemented in that form ☐

3. Discussion tactics

11. Playing 'devil's advocate' ☐

12. Thinking ourselves into their shoes ☐

13. Undermining their arguments: querying the facts/assumptions/conclusions ☐

14. Amplifying weaknesses in the argument and why related issues have been omitted ☐

15. Projecting the consequences if their argument is accepted ☐

16. Undermining their credibility by attacking their self-confidence ☐

17. Inferring that they are out of touch with their own employees ☐

18. Comparing their ideas unfavourably with those of a person they are known to respect ☐

19. Enhancing own arguments and credibility ☐

20. Minimizing own weaknesses ☐

4. Proposing and bargaining

21. Using 'trial proposals' ('Supposing we did x, could you do y?') ☐

22. Offering a 'sprat' to catch the 'mackerel' ☐

23. Pressurizing on time deadlines/mental exhaustion, etc. ☐

24. Reducing their committed position by emphasizing your 'generous movement' ☐

25. Changing the negotiators to break deadlock ☐

5. Closing the deal

26. Trying to get agreement now to save yet more meetings ☐

27. Using the 'one last objection' close ☐

28. Using an extra 'minor inducement' for agreement *now* ☐

29. Using the 'walk-out' ☐

30. Confirming the offer in writing ☐

Now add the new actions and commitments to your personal action plan.

PUSH, PULL AND THE EFFECT OF PERSONALITY

Push and pull are two styles of persuasion commonly used in verbal discussion and their use depends a good deal on the personality involved. Typical **extroverts** just cannot help themselves: when asked a question, they can tend to 'over-answer' by offering too much information. (This style may be the mark of sales and marketing professionals – and, when uncontrolled, has the disadvantage that it may lead to their clients being able to spot more arguments *not* to go ahead with a proposal or to respond with more counter-proposals.)

By contrast, **introverts** may need quite a lot of persuasion to expose their inner thoughts – and, at the extreme end (e.g. very shy people), they can create considerable discomfort to extroverts if they:

- fail to give enough information to support their case

- give one-word answers

- are economical (in the extreme) when responding to small talk.

Sometimes, negotiators rush to judgement in seeking the catches or risks in a scheme or proposal and may become more concerned about feelings than facts. On the other hand, caution is good – especially in the search for facts and evidence that a proposed scheme will work, trouble-free, or that a client really does have the means to settle a bill.

COACHING SESSION 55

Your interaction style: push

Assess whether your interaction style is 'push' by answering these questions.

1. Are you often the first person to talk to fill silences in a discussion (or in a bus queue, doctor's waiting room, etc.)? ☐

   How could you change this?

   _____

   _____

2. Are you someone who talks fluently – with more information supporting arguments than is strictly necessary? ☐

   What effect is this likely to have on your opponent?

   _____

   _____

How could you control this?

_____

_____

3. Do you have long conversations to catch up with news and/or do you have larger than average phone bills? ☐

4. Do you overrun in meetings with colleagues, in job interviews or when brainstorming? ☐

How could you adapt your normal conversation style and gain advantage from a negotiating style?

_____

_____

_____

Make a commitment today to modify your push style of interaction when negotiating. **Make notes in your personal action plan.**

Now assess how the push style might apply in *your* situation.

5. What would be the risks/advantages of a push style in your negotiations with the following?

Suppliers:

_____

_____

Clients:

_____

_____

Advisers:

_____

_____

6. In a situation with extroverts, how could you disentangle yourself politely?

_____

_____

_____

COACH'S TIP

Improve communication

For more effective communication, empathize with your opponent by matching their language style (speed and complexity); clarify your objectives and intentions at the start and keep them in mind; and don't forget to obtain feedback.

COACHING SESSION 56

Your interaction style: pull

Assess your interaction style by answering these questions. If you answer yes to them, your style is more 'pull' than 'push'.

1. Do you prefer to pose open questions (beginning with What? When? Where? How much? and Why?)?
2. Do you listen to others without interrupting or competing for airtime?
3. Do you use silence to encourage others to keep talking?

These might seem to be positive ways of interacting, but take care: asking 'Why?' can sometimes sound aggressive; and using silence can be a discomforting tactic that might lead to an overreaction, and should be used only in extreme situations (e.g. when an unacceptable proposal has been made and the person who has made it needs time to conclude that it is unacceptable).

HIDDEN PERSUADERS

Awareness of all the techniques contained in the previous two coaching sessions is useful in helping to explain what can go well (or badly) in a discussion, but this does not throw much light on *why* a person might appear to be bringing up the wrong issues, arguments or tactics to the meeting. The fact is that we are all flawed in some way as a result of our upbringing, education and life experiences. Usually, we manage to conceal these flaws at work, but sometimes they break out and become obvious in our reactive behaviour. We become motivated not to achieve a logical outcome but to score a point or gain a superior position – or to suggest that our opponent is out of their depth or even incompetent.

Such games can be potentially self-destructive, and may involve a very determined high achiever who resolves to win every argument and deal, regardless of the consequences of this win/lose approach. As you become an experienced negotiator, you will come across such characters.

Transactional analysis seeks to address these issues, by looking at not *what we say* but *how we say it*. Transactional analysis suggests that there are three mental states:

- Parent

- Adult

- Child

Most negotiators need to be in the Adult mental state and using the Adult style of communication most of the time. Dealing with facts is supposed to be the most adult thing for us to do and, when we are in that frame of mind, one might think that, surely, everyone else would see it that way, too? However, we know that, in everyday life, conversation can all too easily turn into an awkward debate – especially when our discussion touches upon topics that bring strongly held opinions. Typically, we are taught to avoid talking about sensitive topics – politics, religion and sex – especially if we have strong views about them. Failure to follow this advice can turn a moderate discussion into a heated one, drawing on questions of 'who did what to whom' and even 'what should be done to the miscreants'.

Optimists say that we can forge a lasting understanding with others when all problems are discussed openly. We will eventually arrive at a cathartic end point when everyone has exhausted their energies and can respond calmly to the issues with a view to achieving a lasting peace and a mutually agreed and desired goal. However, in business dealings (which may be very long-lasting), the reality is that significant differences between the parties must often be put aside in favour of the potential overall gains (i.e. profit, investment, increased employment, strategic development targets and the like).

Of course, the very fact that a negotiation has become necessary suggests that the parties involved have different views about something. That might lead to a level of disagreement, which might be, for example:

- a simple 'try-on' to see whether better ideas, terms or offers might arise

  This is the principle that 'if you don't ask, you don't get'. This doesn't mean that a persuasive case wasn't needed: the more persuasive it is, the greater the chance of success.

- a more extreme response

  Something like 'Your organization has let us down in a major way and we demand satisfaction' could mean having to give a public apology or compensation, or risking legal action.

This rather more serious situation occurs when something has gone badly wrong and one of the parties seeks redress. It is at this point that individuals (and their companies) can rush to respond without thinking and cause even more trouble. In such a situation, the case needs to be properly considered with a full debate on the circumstances, causes and possible remedies. A key element will be how to learn lessons so that a repetition will not occur.

To resolve a serious disagreement, there are various matters to consider:

- The inconvenience
- The consequences of any future loss (e.g. further business)
- The risk of retaliatory action
- The power of the press (negative publicity and its effect on reputation)
- Loss of management time (in what is a distraction from normal duties)
- Loss of goodwill
- The legal consequences
- Appropriate levels of compensation
- Loss of 'face'

We can see from this list that the process of debate in a negotiation does need to be thorough, especially when we are establishing a new business relationship. We should not presume that the earlier stages of setting up a contract or deal are necessarily vulnerable to all these potential losses but we should be aware of the possibility.

MOTIVATION AND NEGOTIATION

Most, if not all, human activity occurs because we are trying to achieve something. We are motivated by a drive or desire to satisfy our needs and wants and so we use negotiation as a means to attain our objectives. Human needs are many and varied but, in order to understand their effect on negotiation, it is helpful to have some method of classifying them. A useful approach is the 'Hierarchy of Needs' pyramid developed by Abraham Maslow (see below). Maslow suggested that there are a number of levels of human need, and that each new higher level becomes a motivator of behaviour once the lower level of need has been satisfied. He also suggested that:

- there is a definite order of relative strengths and importance of needs
- a satisfied need is no longer a motivator of behaviour.

Needs analysis will suggest a strategy for dealing with your opponent's demands. Maslow's approach suggests that the more successful strategy is likely to be the one that indicates to your opponent that you are going to meet his most basic, unsatisfied need. Failure to understand your opponent's needs is the major reason why negotiations are unsuccessful. When negotiators consider their own needs alone, they are dealing with only half of the negotiation equation. Further, they have lost sight of a most important factor for influencing behaviour.

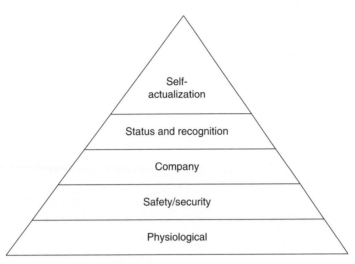

Abraham Maslow's 'Hierarchy of Needs' pyramid

COACH'S TIP

Be aware of motivation

The principle of any negotiation is to satisfy the needs of all parties, which means that the outcome is strongly influenced by the needs and motivation of the parties involved.

COACHING SESSION 57

Needs and negotiation

Look at the following statements about needs and negotiation and answer the questions relating to your own experience and organization.

The purpose of negotiation is needs satisfaction. If people's needs were fully satisfied, there would be no requirement for negotiation.

1. What needs existed when your organization was first formed?

_____

_____

_____

2. How well has it met the needs of its target clients?

_____

_____

3. What needs now exist to help its

- survival?_____

- expansion?_____

- influence?_____

4. How might negotiation skills play a part in achieving these outcomes?

_____

_____

5. What contribution could you make to this process?

_____

_____

6. Make a summary of your ambitions here and add it to your personal action plan.

_____

_____

_____

In a negotiation, both parties have needs. Negotiation presupposes that each party wants something. You have needs you want to satisfy – and so does your opponent.

7. How would you set about discovering the needs of the other party?

_____

_____

8. How might you discover and deal with a hidden agenda?

_____

_____

_____

_____

Negotiators must try to understand their opponent's needs fully, as well as their own. The more you know about your opponent's needs, the more effective a negotiator you will be – because you will be able to determine the best approach to the situation.

9. How would rate yourself on this quality?

100%?	☐
75%?	☐
50%?	☐
25% or less?	☐

If you ticked less than 75%, this issue should be on your action plan.

 COACH'S TIP

Understand your opponents' needs

Opponents act for their reasons – not yours! Understanding their reasons – and their needs – is what lies at the heart of professional negotiation skills.

There are two main types of negotiation:

- Inter-personal (between people)
- Inter-group (between and within organizations)

Organizations do not act independently, but through people. So, in inter-group negotiation, two levels of needs are operating:

- The group needs of the organization
- The personal needs of the individual

For a win/win deal, both levels must be taken into account by negotiators when planning a strategy.

NON-COMMERCIAL NEGOTIATION

Non-commercial negotiation is when advisers and consultants to business or other organizations spend time with individuals and groups to negotiate on proposed changes that will affect them. These changes may be to do with:

- the skills and knowledge base
- working practices
- systems and procedures
- terms and conditions

- opportunities, markets or supplies
- training and people development.

Advisers have responsibilities both to the individuals and groups they work with and also to the organization employing them. Much of their activity does not involve making commercial decisions, as in marketing or procurement, but it may incur considerable costs in terms of resources, time and effort; and the pay-offs may not be easily measured in terms of sales or profit.

The person with ultimate authority and responsibility for taking action and managing change in an organization is often not immediately available to an adviser or consultant, whose first negotiation may be over access and reservation of time in the diary. This means that the adviser must build and maintain relationships in order to benefit the client (the person with the vision of moving from a present to a future position, as shown in the following diagram).

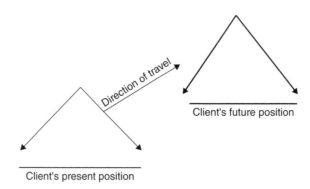

The adviser model

The adviser's role

Advisers need to work with their clients to:

- help diagnose their present position
- develop a vision of the future (including an awareness of the pay-off from moving to this position)
- contribute to, and help manage, the process of change.

They bring knowledge and experience to the relationship but they also need to be able to manage the *process* issues, by:

- being aware of the impact they will have on the client
- developing and maintaining the relationship in order to make it more effective.

It is vital for the adviser to gain the client's acceptance not only of the goals but also the best means of achieving them – the direction of travel – in preference to other options. This will often depend on the level of trust that has developed between adviser and client. As an adviser, how well would this model reflect your priorities in the relationship with your clients?

⚇ COACHING SESSION 58

Your role as adviser

If you have, or plan to take on, this challenging role, answer the following questions.

1. How will you interpret the future for your clients with a 'road map' and strategy for achieving their objectives?

_____

_____

_____

_____

2. What changes in the relationship with your clients would be desirable if they are to achieve maximum benefit from your inputs?

_____

_____

_____

_____

3. How negotiable are these changes, and what could be an effective change agent for generating a more productive relationship?

_____

_____

_____

_____

The adviser needs to address process and task issues:

- Process issues concern what is happening in the relationship and the negotiation's impact on the relationship.
- Task issues concern the client's present position, how the client can manage the change and the future vision (i.e. the pay-off).

Generating support for change in the advisory environment can be expressed in the following equation:

$$\text{Change} = A \times B \times C \times D$$

where:

A = dissatisfaction with present

B = desire for a new situation

C = ease of taking the first step

D = total cost (time, money, effort).

Any one of these factors can seriously reduce the client's willingness and motivation to start on the change journey. The adviser's input needs to recognize the point at which the desire for change is high – and preferably growing (so that positions X and Y on the graph in Coaching session 59 will bring productive returns on advisers' time and effort).

ΩΩ COACHING SESSION 59

The adviser model and change

The graph here shows an organization's internally felt levels of security.

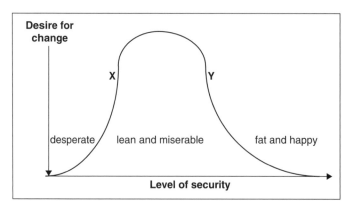

This model indicates that the opportunity for encouraging change is more likely to be to be successful at point X than at point Y, when the organization and senior executives may feel a little complacent. Therefore a change strategy could be different at points X and Y: point X would be an opportunity for vision building, whereas point Y would offer a chance of creating dissonance.

1. How well would this model reflect your priorities as an adviser in establishing a productive relationship with your client?

2. How could a change strategy at points X and Y work in your environment?

3. If your negotiations are targeted to help with (or generate) change, how could you adopt and introduce this concept?

4. How does this concept explain why some organizations are averse to change?

THE DEBATING PROCESS

After the ice-breaking phase of the meeting, it should move naturally into the ebb and flow of a discussion. This progressive step will be affected by, among other things, the time either party has allocated to the meeting (or cycle of meetings). This information is often a key factor in influencing what can be achieved. In these days of concern with individual productivity, time and stress management, all parties will have priorities to meet and the negotiation meeting is just one episode in the parties' lives.

Put into this kind of context, it is easier to understand how things can go wrong. For example:

- the start of the meeting may be delayed by the overrunning of a previous one

- objectives may be affected by other negotiations, which have yet to be resolved

- interruptions may occur, through progress or obstacles being encountered in arrangements with related schemes, deals or suppliers/clients.

In each case, such difficulties may be attributable to the inefficiencies of the appropriate negotiator – or perhaps the disorganization of the business – but the fast-moving nature of the marketplace makes the scenario endemic to business arrangements in the sector. So, it is important for the players to set some goals for the meeting alongside an understanding of the amount of time that can be made available.

There is a significant difference between skilled and average negotiators in the effort they put into preparing for a negotiation. Their perception, incisive grasp of the issues and persuasive style of discussion can make all the difference in the early stages of the meeting (i.e. before concrete proposals are offered, debated and agreed).

COACHING SESSION 60

Reviewing your debating process

Ask yourself the following questions.

1. Did we get all the issues on the table and debate them adequately? Did we miss anything and, if so, what?

_____

_____

2. Could our timing be improved? If so, in what way?

_____

_____

3. How successful were we in drawing out information (e.g. by asking open questions)?

_____

_____

4. How effectively did we all listen to each other?

_____

_____

5. How effective was our signalling (e.g. of flexible positions)

_____

_____

6. How well was discussion controlled (i.e. kept on target/not verbose/no distractions)?

_____

_____

7. How well did we seek movement?

_____

_____

8. How effective was our use of summaries?

_____

_____

9. How could we improve in the future, in terms of all these factors?

_____

_____

_____

_____

_____

THE PROD-ProSC MAP

The PROD-ProSC framework emphasizes the value of open discussion of key agenda issues *before* proposals are made. This helps avoid risks arising from hasty (and ill-thought-out) ideas leading to mistakes and reduces the risk of conceding too much to the other party.

Stage	Issues
P = Prepare	
a) People	Who am I meeting? With what authority?
	Who else is likely to be present?
	What do I know about the culture and style of representatives of this business?
b) Place	Where will we meet? Home or away?
	What is the meeting room like?
	How can I make the communications work for me?
	How affected am I likely to be by the personal comfort factors?
R = Research	What do we know about the trend of deals in this sector?
	How might this affect our goals?
	Have I a clear shopping list of objectives and parameters worked out for each one?
	What could be our opponents' position?
	How could I find out in advance?
	Who might have the power in this relationship?
	How could it be used for mutual benefit?
O = Open	How should I open the meeting?
	What ice-breaking topics might be used?
	Are there any probing questions I could ask? How could we establish some common ground?

D = Debate and discuss	**What style of conversation should I adopt? Competitive/co-operative/consensual/?** **What kind of response are these likely to bring?**
Pro = Propose	How will I resist the temptation to move too quickly/slowly? How could trial proposals help? How will I ensure that all *my proposals* are conditional? What if we have a major disagreement? How will we manage any conflicts?
S = Summarize	How good am I at using summaries in meetings? How will I remember to use summaries during and at the end of the meeting?
C = Close	Who will be responsible for tracking progress at the meeting and at the end? How can I ensure that appropriate notes are taken and that they are accurate and complete? How strong is my decision-making ability? What methods of closing can I use most effectively? If my authority is challenged, how will I manage this?

Once you have explored your current stage, note in your action plan any areas that might need more attention.

NEXT STEPS

You have now seen how open debate and discussion are essential elements of the negotiation process if we are to avoid making proposals that are too hastily agreed. The next part of the process concerns the proposals themselves.

The following chapter discusses how, before moving towards a final agreement, we can make trial proposals. These will help to keep the momentum going and allow us to test for gaps and errors. Then we can progress to carefully worded conditional or unconditional proposals that cover all the important factors.

👍 TAKEAWAYS

What improvements would you like (reflecting on your recent/current negotiations) at work?

_____

_____

_____

_____

_____

What improvements would you like (reflecting on your recent/current negotiations) in your domestic/social life?

_____

_____

_____

_____

_____

Who else is involved in these events and processes?

_____

_____

_____

_____

_____

How would you measure the improvements you would like to achieve at work?

_____

_____

_____

_____

_____

_____

How would you measure the improvements you would like to achieve in your domestic/ social life?

_____

_____

_____

_____

_____

What additional support would be helpful? Who could provide it?

_____

_____

_____

_____

_____

7 | MAKING PROPOSALS

 OUTCOMES FROM THIS CHAPTER

- Understand the importance of proposals in moving negotiations forward towards a final agreement.
- Know how trial proposals can help negotiators achieve movement and avoid deadlock.
- Know the difference between conditional and unconditional proposals.
- Understand the need for testing for gaps in a meeting to avoid exceptions or mistakes.
- Realize how careful wording can ensure flexibility before agreement is finally obtained.

So far, we have emphasized a relatively relaxed approach to negotiation – based on a carefully prepared case – with a meeting that comprises an informal discussion in which the dialogue moves along towards a satisfactory conclusion. But what does that really mean?

If real agreement is to be achieved, at some point the language used needs to become more precise and defined, so that the proposal outlines are clear to all parties and there is no room for misunderstandings. Lack of precision runs the risk that the details of the agreement – and even the contract – will be faulty, leading to recriminations and the need for yet more negotiation. While the earlier stages of a negotiation are important for exchanging ideas, they are important only as preliminaries to producing formal proposals that can be implemented. But who is going to start up this process?

FROM A CHAT TO A DEAL

There are no rules about who should set the pace for these late stages of the meeting: the benefits of being the first person to move the discussion towards the goal can be weighed pretty equally with the benefits of being able to listen and analyse what is being proposed. The purpose of listening to the discussion of the proposal rather than instigating it is that you can more easily spot whether the proposal is leaving out something on your 'wanted' list or whether the summary of what has been discussed has left something out which you consider to be crucial. Whoever makes the first move towards the proposal must correctly build on the exchanges so far and include all the important factors that have been discussed and informally agreed.

COACHING SESSION 61

Forgetting key factors

Have you *ever* agreed a deal and, afterwards, discovered that you did not include an important factor that was on your 'list of needs'?

1. Record it here and state how it happened:

_____

_____

_____

_____

_____

A mark of the exhausted negotiator can be seen in one-way proposals. For example: 'If we purchase this vehicle from you today at this price, then we'd also want a service contract.'

Clearly, this would be a great deal for the buyer if he or she buys the vehicle *with a* service contract thrown in. We do not have the benefit of earlier exchanges, but it sounds as if the result will be win/lose for the vendor. If this is a negotiation, then it could have been much better balanced.

2. Draft your alternative phrasing of the above statement here:

_____

_____

_____

Now compare your version with the draft in the online resource. This revised version might be viewed as lose/win by the vendor but it has made clear that the client is aiming for a better balance between the two sides.

It is easy to make an error at this stage and, possibly, through mishearing or misunderstanding, to agree a deal which, in the cold light of day, turns out to be a poor result, caused by a lack of attention and/or care.

Leading on the proposal

Assess your skills to lead the proposal by considering which of the following behaviours you are best at:

- Forming attractive proposals

- Listening and analysing the offers (against your needs and plan)

When all is considered, negotiators really need to have *both skills* – but you may be more comfortable in one role than the other.

The reactions of your opponent may guide you as to the acceptability of a proposal. For example, if a car dealer were to seek to close a deal hastily, with over-excited words and a handshake, you would be alerted to the fact that maybe the deal is benefiting him rather more than you, the customer.

COACH'S TIP

Recognize a proposal

It is vital to be able to distinguish proposals from more general discussion – since only proposals can be contracted. It is important not to give your opponent the idea that you are ready to propose when all you are doing is 'thinking aloud'.

Read the conversation in the following case study, in which three friends try to reach agreement on how to spend their day off.

CASE STUDY: THREE FRIENDS

1. Jo: I'm planning to go to the coast on that holiday Monday.

2. Helga: Oh, no! We went there last time and it rained all day; can't we do something different?

3. Jo: But the last holiday was in the winter – it's not surprising it rained and current forecasts give us sunshine all day.

4. Abdul: Well, I'd love to come but I am behind with my thesis. I cannot afford the time – and, anyway, the car needs a new tyre and I've no cash.

5. Jo: I thought you were up to date – wasn't that why you asked me to help you last month? It's supposed to be your own work, you know!

6. Abdul: Yeah, I know that – but it's not that easy when the language isn't your home language. I think I'll pack this course in and go home.

7. Helga: You can't do that – you'll lose your deposit on the flat and we can't afford to pay your rent as well as our own.

8. Abdul: That's all you care about, isn't it? (*making for the door*) You guys can hand me back the deposit I paid; no doubt you'll get another one from my replacement. I think I'll head off to the travel agent and get a plane ticket straight away.

9. Jo: Don't be so hasty! Think about your career – and how your government would see your throwing away the chance of the degree here.

10. Helga: And your father wouldn't be impressed – you told us that he's made a lot of sacrifices to get you here. If you're feeling that distracted, go and see your tutor. I did that last term and found her very helpful…

11. Abdul: I don't want her knowing my business – but I suppose I could go and see the department head – he's always saying he's here to help.

13. Jo: Yeah – but he's not of this world – lives on Cloud Nine – you'll be better off talking to the student counsellor in the Students' Union.

14. Helga: Hey! What about your girlfriend? She'll be devastated if you go. See, it's a decision full of complications. Please don't do anything rash!

15. Abdul: Thanks, guys, it's good to know you care – how about you lending me the money to get my car back on the road, then? Then we could all go to the coast together!

16. All: (*Laughter*)

COACHING SESSION 62

What is a proposal?

In the heat of a negotiation, it can be easy to lose sight of how well (or not) the conversation is progressing. This session asks you to analyse the case study for the common behaviours we all use and rate them for their value in progressing the meeting's objectives.

1. Grade each interaction as follows:

   A = progressing the meeting towards an agreed outcome
   C = potentially obstructing agreement

When you have finished, check your answers with the analysis in the online resources for this chapter.

2. Now reread the conversation and complete a more detailed analysis using the following breakdown:

   GI = Giving information

   TP = Trial proposal

   Dis = Disagreeing

   Prop = Proposing

   Sum = Summarizing

O = Open

Sup = Supporting

TU = Testing understanding

D/A = Defence/Attack

SI = Seeking information

Abdul might seem to be quite manipulative in this interaction. The principle of avoiding a negotiation when the agenda is not entirely clear may be rather obvious. However, no matter how hard we try to prepare for a negotiation meeting, there is always the possibility of something unexpected. The danger is that it can be very easy to 'give an issue away'. This may seem unimportant or inexpensive at the meeting but it could prove to be very expensive later on.

COACH'S TIP

Clarify your agenda

Do this by spending more time in preparation. Also, if unexpected items are raised at the meeting, call a break so that checks can be made; or break off and arrange another meeting after you have checked out the new idea or data.

Using the 'if...then' formula

The best approach to use for negotiations is where actions by one party are linked directly to actions by the other side. This typically means using the formula:

'**If** we accept this price you have quoted, **then** will you deliver it at no extra cost by this coming weekend?'

There is a matter of trust involved here – but payment agreed (and paid up-front) could put the buyer in a weak position if the delivery is delayed (or, worse, not made at all).

Giving information

The most common behaviour in a meeting is giving information (GI). This may or may not be accompanied by emotions or a persuasive tone, and it may also be lacking in facts. Giving too much information can lead to 'overload' that is exhausting for the other party – and may even lose you a possible contract.

The behaviour of top negotiators

It would be a mistake to think that everyone who is trusted to negotiate on behalf of their group or organization is already good at the top behaviours that help build an agreement. As a negotiator yourself, you should know your strengths and weaknesses and, from your experience, you'll remember all those you have worked with who have proved to be excellent negotiators (possibly even better than you).

Behaviours used by top negotiators when making proposals are as follows:

1. **Building** on others' ideas
2. **Supporting** other people's ideas and proposals
3. **Testing understanding** (clarifying helps to avoid misunderstandings)
4. **Presenting** information **assertively**
5. **Signalling** that it is time to move the discussion forward
6. **Forming and using proposals** to progress the meeting

The critical factor that makes these behaviours successful is that they are balanced between talking and listening.

Behaviours to avoid

And here's a list of behaviours to be avoided, or at least controlled:

1. **Counter-proposals** (unless your sector of business is known for haggling, in which case this will be a valued skill)
2. **Defence/attack** (which can lead to 'tit-for-tat' exchanges that spiral out of control)
3. **Blocking** and stating difficulties (which can generate significant frustration in opponents and reduce the wish to be supportive with more generous offers)
4. **Accepting inadequacy** or fault (this is not about appearing to be 'perfect' but just not committing 'own goals' in front of your opponents).
5. **Shutting other people out** (usually by talking too much, ignoring other people's interactions or becoming 'deaf').

COACHING SESSION 63

Analysing behaviour

A common fault in negotiations is that there is too much talking and too little disciplined listening – leading to misunderstandings at best and conflict at worst. The following conversation might be heard in a meeting between a heating contractor and a householder. Using the behaviours listed above, match each sentence to one type of behaviour. The householder starts with a 'typical' signal…

Speaker	Words spoken	Behaviour type
Householder:	Goodness, where do we go from here? It's a lot more complicated than I had imagined.	
Contractor:	Yes, I agree. But all the options can really be narrowed down to the decision about whether to change power source or not. Which is not such a big issue, as you'll see when we look at the various projections of your future bills! How do you feel about solar panels?	
Householder:	Well, I think they are a great way forward – the system for the future – but…	
Contractor:	Why don't I work out a quick ballpark figure for you? It won't take long.	
Householder:	There wouldn't be any obligation on me to accept, would there? I'd need to have any formal quote checked over by my family.	
Contractor:	Oh! I thought you had made a request for a visit to make a change to your fuel account! I haven't got time to waste on speculative enquiries. Give me a call when you're ready to go ahead. Good day!	

The model answers and a commentary are in the online resources.
Go to www.TYCoachbooks.com/Negotiation

 COACH'S TIP

Listen and ask questions

Enthusiastic extroverts or 'dominant dictators' often want to tell their opponents what to do (which can create considerable defence barriers). If this is you, you need to improve your listening skills and try to engage in conversations by asking more questions and listening to the answers. A low-key question might draw an opponent out: 'We've talked through quite a lot of detail now and I'm wondering if it's time to agree on working together?'

USING POSITIVE TECHNIQUES

Here is a list and brief description of the key factors that can help to turn average meetings into high-achieving ones. Even if they are not new to you, take this opportunity to reconsider them and commit to putting them to frequent use – since practice makes perfect.

- **Signalling**

  In many negotiation meetings (or telephone calls), proposing often results from a natural, flowing conversation. However, there are occasions when neither side seems ready or able to progress to this state, so a signal can help to concentrate minds and move the meeting along.

- **Making concessions**

  By making a 'special offer' that is available for only a limited time, negotiators are often able to motivate opponents to progress the meeting towards a deal.

- **Checking for reactions**

  Drawing out people's reactions by asking questions will give you insight into what they are really thinking. For example, ask 'Is this the kind of scheme/product/service you had in mind?'

- **Taking a break (recess)**

  Most negotiators like to think that they have greatest influence when their opponent is in front of them. But taking a break from the negotiating table allows everyone to relax a little from the intense concentration required. (NB: Don't expect a competitive advantage from this: you are *both* having the break!)

COACHING SESSION 64

Signalling

There are various ways to signal to your opponent that you are ready to move on.

How would you phrase such a signal? Draft two alternative approaches appropriate to your own business/organization here:

1. _____

   _____

2. _____

   _____

COACHING SESSION 65

Concessions and 'packages'

We are all familiar with the special offer or 'package' that is only available now/today/this week. Negotiators are often able to use such ideas or schemes to motivate opponents to progress the meeting towards a conclusion. (This type of approach can be habit forming, however, and may lead your opponent to expect the same treatment next time.)

Draft two concessions that should not lead your opponent to expect the same treatment next time:

1. _____

_____

_____

2. _____

_____

_____

COACHING SESSION 66

Checking for reactions

If you have been the prime mover in the meeting so far, you may need to draw out some more reactions – which probably means asking questions to try to draw out the client's inner thoughts and plans. It is essential that you look and listen hard for (positive) reactions.

In this case, draft your question and the type of answer you would hope to receive:

Question:

_____

_____

Desired answer:

_____

_____

Types of recess

There are two types of recess:

- **The conversational recess**

  Combined with a 'refreshment offer', this allows for a change of topic and a general chat (taking care not to lead into any controversy that could cause disagreement between the sides). This tactic can also provide a useful break in a meeting if you need to diffuse tension or distract attention from an error or a negative point.

  For example: '...That reminds me, did you see that thing on the News last night about the possible world shortage of oysters in Patagonia? Would you ever believe that?'

- **The physical recess**

  Providing a side room for the opposing team to reflect on the discussion so far (or to check that their brief has not been compromised) is a healthy facility. It might be tempting for the host to eavesdrop on the discussion – but this risks the whole enterprise if the team discovers that this has happened.

While recesses can be very useful, they are not without the potential for 'traps' and misunderstandings. While such a distraction gives you an opportunity to reflect and re-enter the negotiation with a preferential progress summary, this could also be misused and seen as a trick by the other side. Be vigilant and aware of this tactic in case it is practised against you.

COACHING SESSION 67

Taking a break or recess

A break or recess may be a good plan for all parties to a negotiation. It offers a chance for people to catch up with emails or take an urgent call – and also allows them to relax after the intense concentration required during the negotiation.

1. How would you use a conversational recess? Write a step-by-step plan here:

   a) _____

   b) _____

   c) _____

   d) _____

   e) _____

2. What might be the potential risks of a conversational recess?

_____

_____

_____

_____

3. What kind of information is most likely to be influential in a conversational recess?

_____

_____

_____

_____

4. How would you use a physical recess? Write a step-by-step plan here:

a) _____

b) _____

c) _____

d) _____

e) _____

5. What might be the potential risks of a physical recess?

_____

_____

_____

_____

6. How will you be certain to restart at a point consistent with the situation before the break?

_____

_____

_____

_____

TYPES OF PROPOSAL

In reality, proposals are the only behaviour that move a negotiation forward – and it is easy to see why it can take some time before either (or both) parties feel ready to trade proposals. What is happening up to that point is building trust and ensuring that nothing is 'given away', for little or no return. For this reason, these classifications should make it much easier to interpret progress in the meeting; your listening skills are crucial!

There are five kinds of proposal: process, content, trial, conditional and counter-proposals.

1. **The process proposal**

    These are usually suggestions on how the meeting might progress and, on the whole are not threatening, unless you wish to dominate the meeting with your own methods, sequence, etc. and nothing else will do. (If this is the case, return to the advice in Chapter 1.)

2. **The content proposal**

    As the name suggests, this is any proposal that is about the subject being debated. Ideally, it will emerge as 'conditional' (see below).

3. **The trial proposal**

    Some discussions don't move forward because neither party seems able to make the required move – maybe for fear of making a mistake. In such a situation, trial proposals provide a useful, positive 'nudge'. What they say is: 'I am feeling almost ready to do a deal – but only if you feel the same.'

    Trial proposals are also easier to withdraw if they are queried or if, on reflection, sound inadequate: 'Suppose we were able to ... we might then find a way to progress to a new specification.'

4. **The conditional proposal**

    The most important technique used by skilled negotiators is the formation of conditional proposals. This means indicating that the proposals are conditional on the other party's action: 'If you are prepared to order the product in boxes of 10 and accept our minimum quantities, then we would accept your price proposal.'

5. **The counter-proposal**

    A feature of competitive negotiators is their wish to have the last word and this can cause the proposing phase of a negotiation to become almost an auction or bidding war. There is nothing dangerous or misleading in a period of counter-proposing (but the technique may feel like the kind of bargaining more suited to the marketplace). In the Western world, people tend to prefer to do business in a rather more sophisticated way and may become irritated by negotiators who constantly look for a better deal for them – regardless of your needs.

When to use a trial proposal

Inexperienced negotiators often have difficulty in progressing a meeting from the maze of discussion towards the 'finishing line' of a deal. They find it hard to piece together the issues and are uncertain of how to gain their objectives without making unnecessarily expensive concessions. Trial proposals provide the best route forward for tentative negotiators. They are a way of 'testing the water' without making a final commitment, or 'jumping in at the deep end'.

After a discussion around the topic, the sharing of points of view and the exchange of information, the moment will be right to move the negotiation forward. Don't get to the stage when the players keep repeating more or less the same things to each other, since this is likely to end in frustration all round.

The term 'trial' indicates that proposals offered in this way are attempts to find out whether the other party is ready (or can be persuaded) to move forward, but without committing themselves. It could be thought of as a kind of 'tease':

- 'Well, suppose we were able to, would you consider it a possibility for you to...?'

- 'How would you feel if, maybe, we could deliver the new stock order next month – provided we had this outstanding account cleared beforehand?' (pause)

- 'Let's imagine that there was no recession, we'd both have a nice fat balance in the bank and no bad debts ... how would it be if we were to introduce a special supplier scheme – discounting cash payments on an attractive scale? Would you be interested in opening a supply account with us?'

Because these proposals are tentative, they allow for the possibility that they could be improved or rejected – or even accepted. There would still be a chance of revising the proposal by either side if it is unacceptable or, perhaps, thought to be ungenerous. The technique teases out the possibilities without concrete commitment from either side. If both sides agree without any further changes, then the next step would be to summarize with a formal, 'If... then' proposal – which should lead to acceptance and agreement.

When to use a conditional proposal

Avoid proposals that are not linked to any conditions. In other words, don't give anything away without getting something in return; it is a bad principle and encourages opponents to think that you are a soft bet. The vital point here is that a concession or offer is available to the other party *only* if certain conditions are met – that is, it is something for something (the quid pro quo).

Proposals become more concrete as they are pieced together in the meeting and as the agenda is progressed. Naive negotiators may become confused at this stage and find themselves using another (mistaken) form of proposal, such as: 'If we could place these larger orders, then we could also put them on display in the new branches we have just taken over.' This is obviously not a quid pro quo and it could lead to a very poor deal.

COACHING SESSION 68

Phrasing different types of proposal

The different types of proposal described above need to be expressed in different ways. Your wording of each of these types of proposal will also depend on the case and the situation.

Using a recent project, write typical proposals for each of the five categories here:

1. Process:

_____

_____

2. Content:

_____

_____

3. Trial:

_____

_____

4. Conditional:

_____

_____

5. Counter:

_____

_____

COACH'S TIP

Choose the right kind of proposal

Use a trial (or tentative) proposal if you are unsure whether you have full agreement of your opponent. Use a conditional proposal to 'cement' action agreed by both parties.

Considering a counter-proposal

When assertive negotiators see an opportunity to gain control of the meeting, their natural response will be to counter your proposal(s) with something different almost immediately. This indicates a very competitive style, and lower-key negotiators should be aware that this could lead to a win/lose result against them. That is not to say that the merits of the counter-proposal should not be considered, but that any pressure to accept should be steadfastly resisted until the consequences have been weighed up.

A highly competitive meeting is likely to move fast and with quite a lot of excitement, even tinged with aggression. In this scenario you will need to consider carefully the potential consequences of any agreement to prevent later regrets over acceptance of a one-sided deal. (This is why some business sectors always provide a standard 'cooling-off period'.)

Most players using this technique are not only highly competitive but will have already given plenty of hints about their proposal and closing methods in earlier parts of the discussion.

COACHING SESSION 69

Responding to counter-proposals

How would you respond to a counter-proposal?

Write down five possible responses here:

1. _____

_____

2. _____

_____

3. _____

_____

4. _____

_____

5. _____

_____

LINKING ISSUES TOGETHER

Linking issues together is natural for all negotiators and the starting point lies in the preparation of a 'list of needs', as discussed in Chapter 5. At the discussion stage, each party can seek to assemble the needs of the opposite party – so that costs can be assessed against value (or opportunity) with regard to the needs of each side. Using a domestic house move as an example, a vital part of the estate agent's role would be to establish clearly what is and is not included in the sale.

While many negotiations take place around seemingly simple commercial decisions (buying and selling things such as homes, cars, suites of furniture, etc.), a great many deals are completed over non-financial topics, when success or failure is much less easy to measure. For example:

- a trade union may have worked hard to increase its membership as a means of gaining recognition from an employer who had previously rejected all its claims on the grounds that it did not represent many of the employees

- a staff association may foresee a need for improved security lockers in staff cloakrooms (when the facility is no longer adequate) and seek ideas and reactions from staff representatives

- an airline might wish to sponsor a charity to help promote its image as a caring organization and seek applications from various charity representatives to find the one(s) with the most parallel opportunities (e.g. countries of operation, generation or health needs).

THE IMPORTANCE OF PRESENTATION

The proposal stage is the time when a negotiator's credibility is most at stake. You may have made a proposal but be thinking, 'If I were in their shoes, would I accept it?' and wanting to answer, 'Certainly not!' It might just be your first of many proposals – and possibly just a tester – but any non-verbal signal from you (like scratching your head, rubbing your eye or tugging at your ear) may indicate your discomfort and encourage your opponent to reject or even attack your proposal.

You also need to ask:

- How would this client view our competitors' reputation?
- How reliable have they proved – generally?
- Who is on their client list?
- What authority would they bring to a meeting?
- How would the individuals impress and how trustworthy do they appear to be?
- How might costings compare?

Your non-verbal communication

Physical behaviour needs to be consistent to support the proposals stage (especially if your opponent has avoided showing any commitment so far). Ensure that you do not unwittingly give opponents reasons not to commit, by asking yourself how easily you are able to do the following:

- Be natural and control your nerves
- Maintain eye contact
- Look/maintain a poised position (sitting or standing)
- Control hands/fingers/head position and avoid fidgeting
- Choose appropriate business clothes (dress to impress)
- Use ordinary language
- Speak at a steady pace, using pauses
- Maintain a level voice tone
- Take care with pitch, volume and modulation
- Encourage client involvement (and not be too pushy)
- Maintain enthusiasm, energy and excitement
- Take care with humour (avoid the risk of upsetting opponents with inappropriate stories or jokes)
- Make special efforts with names – your team and theirs!
- Take care with aids (laptop illustrations, documentation, graphs, etc.).

COACHING SESSION 70

Improving your non-verbal communication

Here is an opportunity to reflect on what you can do to improve your non-verbal communication.

1. If your opponent fails to observe any of the behaviours listed above, what effect does it convey to you?

_____

_____

_____

_____

2. Have you carried out a negotiation exercise and had it video recorded? If so, how happy were you with your performance?

_____

_____

_____

_____

3. Write down here how you might improve in this respect and add it to your personal action plan.

_____

_____

_____

_____

_____

_____

LISTENING SKILLS

While many negotiators will have received some training in their careers on how to put a presentation together and deliver it, rather fewer of us have been taught about listening – and yet this is crucial to the process of negotiation.

We are all guilty of poor listening from time to time – and some of us never seem to get any better at it – but in negotiation it is a potentially serious disability. This is especially true if we are working with an opponent who sends signals and hints indicating flexibility, preferential rates and side benefits, etc. – but which are available only if you actively ask for them to be built into the package deal.

Poor listening skills are something we are usually completely unaware of. Active listening is demanding because it asks us to:

- pay full attention to and analyse what we are being told

- put this information alongside known facts and preferences and our strategy

- prepare to format an appropriate response to fit within our prepared negotiation plan – ensuring its suitability, power, influence and likely success.

We must analyse and take into account the manner in which statements are made – which could well affect our considered responses (we become proactive rather than simply reactive). Is it surprising that some people say that they would rather not bother with negotiating?

TRUST AND INTEGRITY

Trust is most commonly at risk when a meeting is progressing well and negotiators are becoming excited. Uncontrolled interaction has benefits, however, as well as disadvantages. It can help to ensure that:

- participants are prepared to discuss any issue that has been accepted as negotiable

- opponent(s) do not lose credibility in the eyes of their team

- the information that has been declared publicly will be used to achieve a formal commitment

- there is no 'trickery' in the final agreement

- a 'final bargain' is implemented in that form (and not used as a new baseline for renegotiation).

Uncontrolled interaction can have unexpected consequences for the proposer that may be less welcome:

- You cannot withdraw an unconditional offer once it is made.

- You cannot deny an offer when it has been unambiguously accepted.

Maintaining trust

When the meeting is going well and feelings of trust are high, you still need to ensure that any negative feelings are minimized and that all the good work is not risked with thoughtless ideas and expressions that may risk the outcome of the negotiation.

All negotiations affect events or plans for the future and therefore could be sensitive, confidential or even secret. They can also be complicated – needing serious concentration and full understanding. Here are some potential weaknesses to be aware of and guard against:

1. **Interrupting**

   Highly competitive negotiators find it hard to stop themselves interrupting the flow of a presentation – especially if they strongly disagree with something that has been said. This can lead to frustration for the other party – especially if the point will be covered later. Some people also have the habit of completing a sentence *before* or *as* the other speaker is finishing – which is also a great irritant.

2. **Selective listening**

   Do you know someone who remembers only what they want to remember? This is probably because they only really hear (and remember) what fits with their plan or ideas! Good negotiators are people who pay attention to everyone's needs – even if some cannot be accommodated in this deal at this time. The best relationships are formed from give-and-take rather than one-way roles.

3. **Not concentrating**

   Concentration levels vary very considerably from person to person – and it would be the mark of a highly competitive host if a meeting were called with a determination to reach agreement, no matter how long it took. (This, of course, assumes that the host has unlimited energy and concentration and is prepared to use this to grind opponents down.)

4. **Making hasty judgements**

   Are you the type of person who tends to make snap judgements about things and people? Or are you constantly challenged by shortage of time so that you feel obliged to make hasty judgements about proposals and the people making them? Maybe history has proved that your instinct is sound but take care: top negotiators who appear to 'cut corners' are nearly always working in their area of expertise.

COACHING SESSION 71

Dealing with your shortcomings

If you are guilty of any of the above four weaknesses, think about how you might overcome them.

To avoid making potentially serious errors, how will you deal with the shortcomings you have identified?

_____

_____

_____

_____

_____

_____

_____

_____

_____

COACHING SESSION 72

Your influencing style

Your personal style of influencing will have been on show long before proposals are being debated in the meeting. However, the nine strategies and tactics commonly used by negotiators and influencers are likely to become obvious as the meeting hits its stride.

Which of them can you identify from your field of work and how could you use them?

1. **INFORMATIONAL:** this style refers to what is actually contained in the communication and not to any quality of the influencer. Who do you know who uses this style?

   Are you a 'content' person? ☐

   Does it work, or are your opponents exhausted by having to do too much listening? Do they agree with you simply to stop the 'earache'?

   _____

What steps will you take to get this under control?

_____

_____

_____

_____

_____

_____

_____

_____

_____

_____

2. **COERCIVE:** this style is based on the ability of the influencer to punish, force or compel. Who do you know who uses this style?

Are you a 'coercive' person (generally and/or in negotiations)? ☐

Are you backed by formal authority or is it simply force of personality?

_____

How do you win yourself a hearing – and does the other person really listen?

_____

_____

_____

_____

What reactions does this style bring out in you?

_____

_____

_____

What actions do you plan to gain more influence in this situation?

_____

_____

_____

_____

_____

_____

_____

_____

_____

_____

3. **REWARD:** this style is based on the ability of the influencer to manipulate rewards, e.g. commission, profit margins, orders, order quantities, deliveries. (Parents often use this bargaining method with their children.) Who do you know who uses this style?

Are you a 'reward' person? ☐

Do you emphasize reward in your persuasion meetings? ☐

When does this style work satisfactorily?

_____

_____

_____

_____

How could you use this approach in your meetings? What steps will you take?

_____

_____

_____

_____

_____

_____

_____

_____

_____

_____

4. **REFERENT:** this style stems from the liking or identification of the influenced with the influencer and can be both a strength and a weakness. We all would prefer to be liked by others, but is it reasonable to expect this to work with everybody? Rejection can hurt some people to the extent that they'll do almost anything to avoid it.

Are you a 'referent' person, highly regarded by your peers and managers? ☐

Do you consciously encourage people to like you? ☐

Do you get upset when they are less influenced than you would prefer? ☐

How could you become more influential?

_____

_____

_____

_____

_____

How could you have your advice accepted more of the time? What steps will you take?

_____

_____

_____

_____

_____

_____

5. **EXPERT**: this style is based on the attribution of superior knowledge or ability to the influencer by the influenced. Who do you know who uses this style?

Does it influence *you*? If so, why, and if not, why not?

_____

_____

_____

_____

What steps would you need to take in order to be able to make credible use of this influencing method?

_____

_____

_____

_____

_____

_____

_____

_____

6. **LEGITIMATE**: this style is based on 'normal styles of behaviour' or 'custom and practice'. For example, if past meetings have 'always taken place in the boardroom' where management benefits are freely available (e.g. coffee, gateaux, drinks), these benefits might not guarantee that negotiations with, for example, trade unionists will be easy or successful – but moving the venue to the works canteen, without consultation, could cause a significant disruption to management/staff relations. Who do you know who uses this style?

Does it influence *you*? If so, why, and if not, why not?

_____

_____

_____

_____

What steps would you need to take in order to be able to make credible use of this influencing method?

_____

_____

_____

_____

_____

_____

_____

_____

7. **COMPLIANCE:** this is where a person accepts influence because it is seen as a way to get the other side to do what is wanted. Put another way, does anyone have a hold over you? Who do you know who uses this style?

How did this loss of 'independence' arise?

_____

_____

_____

How could you dilute it or cancel it out?

_____

_____

_____

_____

Does it influence _you_? If so, why, and if not, why not?

_____

_____

_____

What steps would you need to take in order to be able to make credible use of this influencing method – without the negative after-effects?

_____

_____

_____

_____

_____

_____

_____

_____

8. **IDENTIFICATION:** this is where one person identifies with another and attempts to be like the other person. This may be in terms of dress, appearance, manner of speech and even specific phrases adopted. At the mildest level, this copying behaviour can be flattering – but is best ignored. When it becomes obsessive, which can happen, disaster beckons.

Have you noticed anyone trying to mirror (or borrow) your identity? ☐

Could it ever apply in your situation? ☐

What steps would you need to take in order to be able to make controlled use of this influencing method, without the negative effects?

_____

_____

_____

_____

_____

_____

_____

_____

_____

_____

9. **INTERNALIZATION:** this can occur when we accept another party's influence because we share their values but we remain unaware of what has happened – and thus compromise our freedom as an individual and a negotiator. Extricating oneself from such a position and reasserting one's independence may take time and cause conflict – but in career terms it would be worth it.

Might this approach ever have compromised your position? ☐

Might you have internalized someone else's choice of language, attitudes, performance and/or lifestyle without noticing it? ☐

What steps would you need to take in order to be able to make limited use of this influencing method – without the negative effects?

_____

_____

_____

_____

_____

_____

_____

_____

_____

_____

STYLE MATTERS

Negotiators are very sensitive to other people's negotiating style and will have their likes and dislikes. Being able to go with our preferences, however, is a luxury for most of us: unless we are very fortunate, we have to make the best relationship we can with anyone nominated to do business with us. It is difficult not to prefer some individuals to others but, when such discrimination occurs, there is a risk that decisions become subjective instead of objective, and this is when problems can arise – for example with more business being placed with one supplier or client than with another.

Here are some style issues to consider when you are preparing for your meeting. You could try them out yourself and see who else uses them and how effective they are.

Using persuasive phrases

Some negotiators have perfected this style, which presumes an affirmative decision from the opponent as a natural response to every question.

For example:

- 'It's a nice scheme, **isn't it**?'

- 'It would work well here, **wouldn't it**?'

- 'Your clients could go for it in a big way, **don't you think**?'

- 'So, it will make an obvious follow-up to the present scheme, **won't it**?'

In each case there is an implied suggestion that 'yes' is the best answer to the question.

Suggesting timescales

For most new schemes, there is a best timing available, but such an approach has to be applied and this needs careful discussion – especially if 'on-costs' with less favourable timings are involved. It could be argued that such issues are a luxury when we are seeking to introduce a completely new product or service – which should be the main 'win'. However, the *way* of introducing a new scheme can have a big effect on its market take-up and sales performance, as analysed by neutral observers who are not influenced by either side.

Being assertive

As a negotiation begins to move toward the 'closing', the personalities involved may increase the pressure by deliberately avoiding any verbal or non-verbal signals that their opponents could read as indicating a forthcoming agreement. Specific questioning may help to guard you against any accusations of foot dragging; the 'how, what, when, where and who' approaches will keep you in the game but without having to make an explicit decision before you are ready.

Showing integrity

This important quality will make all the difference to your relationships. Responsible negotiators try to create conditions of trust between the parties involved and they are careful not to embellish the facts or mislead the other side in any way. Without this trust, there is a danger that the implementation step will fail – and even lead to a serious dispute.

🗩🗩 COACHING SESSION 73

Honing your style

What improvements could you make to your negotiating style? Try out the suggestions for increasing success in negotiating, described above, in your next negotiation and record the results here.

Using persuasive phrases

_____

_____

_____

_____

_____

_____

_____

_____

_____

Suggesting timescales

_____
_____
_____
_____
_____
_____
_____

Being assertive

_____
_____
_____
_____
_____
_____
_____
_____

Showing integrity

_____
_____
_____
_____
_____
_____
_____

THE PROD-ProSC MAP

Stage	Issues
P = Prepare	
a) People	Who am I meeting? With what authority?
	Who else is likely to be present?
	What do I know about the culture and style of representatives of this business?
b) Place	Where will we meet? Home or away?
	What is the meeting room like?
	How can I make the communications work for me?
	How affected am I likely to be by the personal comfort factors?
R = Research	What do we know about the trend of deals in this sector? How might this affect our goals?
	Have I a clear shopping list of objectives and parameters worked out for each one?
	What could be our opponents' position?
	How could I find out in advance?
	Who might have the power in this relationship?
	How could it be used for mutual benefit?
O = Open	How should I open the meeting?
	What ice-breaking topics might be used?
	Are there any probing questions I could ask? How could we establish some common ground?
D = Debate and discuss	What style of conversation should I adopt? Co-operative/consensual/competitive?
	What kind of response is this likely to bring?

Pro = Propose	How will I resist the temptation to move too quickly/slowly?
	How could trial proposals help?
	How will I ensure that all my proposals are conditional?
	What if we disagree in a major way?
S = Summarize	How good am I at using summaries in meetings?
	How will I remember to use summaries – during and at the end of the meeting?
C = Close	Who will be responsible for tracking progress at the meeting and at the end?
	How can I ensure that appropriate notes are taken and that they are accurate and complete?
	How strong is my decision-making ability?
	What methods of closing can I use most effectively?
	If my authority is challenged, how will I manage this?

Once you have explored your current stage, note in your action plan any areas that might need more attention.

 ONLINE RESOURCE

More on proposals

The model answers for Coaching sessions 61 to 63 are included in the online resources, along with further advice on strengthening negotiations. Go to:

www.TYCoachbooks.com/Negotiation

NEXT STEPS

You should now have an understanding of the importance of proposals in moving negotiations forward towards a final agreement and how trial proposals can help negotiators continue the conversation and avoid deadlock. You have also learned the difference between conditional and unconditional proposals and how to avoid leaving gaps in the proposal. Careful wording and awareness of style issues can help maintain good relationships so that an agreement that satisfies all parties can be reached.

However, it is always possible that the negotiation fails to reach agreement and even ends in a dispute. The next chapter deals with sources of conflict and how to deal with them.

TAKEAWAYS

Why are proposals important in moving negotiations forward towards a final agreement?

_____

_____

_____

_____

_____

_____

_____

How can trial proposals help negotiators achieve movement and avoid deadlock?

_____

_____

_____

_____

_____

_____

_____

What is the difference between conditional and unconditional proposals?

_____

_____

_____

_____

_____

_____

_____

How can you test for gaps in a meeting to avoid exceptions or mistakes?

_____

_____

_____

_____

_____

_____

_____

What additional support would be helpful to you now? Who could provide it?

_____

_____

_____

_____

_____

_____

_____

8 MANAGING CONFLICT

 OUTCOMES FROM THIS CHAPTER

- Understand how conflict can arise (or be generated through motives) before, during and after a negotiation.

- Identify common sources of conflict.

- Know your options for defusing conflict and seeking satisfactory resolution.

- Understand and avoid the behaviours that can trigger or bolster conflict situations.

Conflict, sadly, often arises in negotiation meetings. Negotiators who have been closely involved in conflict tell of the strong impact it has had on them. Could these experiences colour their attitudes towards negotiation generally, making it (perhaps) more difficult for collaborative bargaining techniques to be developed and applied?

This chapter aims to help you:

- research the root causes and the politics of conflict

- consider the motivators of conflict

- identify the causes of deadlock and how to resolve them.

So far, we have been analysing negotiation skills as they would apply in a commercial setting but the same principles apply to a non-commercial setting. The continuing case study looks at one of a regular series of staff consultative meetings between BuGS management and staff representatives at their Head Office base. The company has not officially recognized a trade union because it is thought that very few staff members are members of (or interested in) any of the national trade unions. It is the management's policy to provide compensation and benefits towards the 'top end' of the building supplies sector – so there seems to be no appetite among the majority of staff for that position to change – except among the firm's delivery drivers, one or two of whom can be quite militant and noisy.

CASE STUDY: BuGS JOINT STAFF CONSULTATIVE MEETING

Purpose of meeting: to brief on the forthcoming introduction of point-of-order terminals (POTs) for all customer orders

Agenda

1. Apologies

2. Minutes of last meeting

3. Matters arising

4. Briefing on the POTs Project from Noel (IT Manager)

5. Any Other Business (incl. Bank Holiday working procedures)

Record of meeting

Present: Sidney (Chair), James (Deputy Manager, Branch 10), Ahmed (Yard Foreman, Head Office Operations), Bob (Driver), Jasmin (Accounts), Jack (Stock Controller), Dot (Sales Clerk), April (Secretary).

1. Chair: Good morning, everyone, and thank you for coming. I know this is a short meeting – but I felt it important to brief you on the plans for these wonderful gadgets that Noel is going to tell us about, which will bring 100-per-cent improvement to our customer service and beat our competitors hands down! I know the grapevine has been very active so here's the chance to get the true story – and it's going to make life so much easier!

2. Bob: I don't know about making life easier! From what I hear, everyone's going to join the union to fight redundancies caused by these new-fangled gizmos. It's a typical management ploy to get the staff numbers down!

3. Chair: That's exactly where you're wrong! Anyway, what's all this talk about a union? This is a strong family business that prides itself on treating staff as part of our extended family. We don't need unions here!

4. Bob: Try telling that to the drivers! Why, only yesterday someone was telling me about his driving hours – they sounded illegal to me.

5. Chair: That's a very serious matter – who are you talking about? I need to get some more details on that...

6. Bob: Well, I don't want trouble; he's a good mate. Leave it there! But it shows how out of touch managers are here.

7. Ahmed and Jack: *(agreeing by nodding and grunting)*

8. Noel: With respect, I have another meeting at 1 o'clock, so would you like me to explain the proposed system?

9. The others: Yes, please!

10. Noel: Well, this little gizmo will be a step-up for our customer service (*waving something looking a little like an iPhone*) because it will enable our sales reps to dial into our stock records, branch by branch, and book the customer's order there and then – with a next-day delivery.

11. Bob: But that presumes the driver can get there the next day – what about when the lorry's off the road?

12. Noel: I can't answer that – it depends on –

13. Bob: See what I mean? We're losing control of everything!

14. Dot: What I want to know is, what's our team going to be doing if the system is taking over our jobs? I've worked here for nearly 20 years and I don't see why we should lose out – me and the other girls! We hate computers – give me *real* people to deal with every time… Why, only the other day –

15. Chair: Don't worry, Dot, we are only talking here about possibilities. The Board hasn't yet signed up for this system – and we're hardly likely to upset you and the girls with all that you've done over the last decades!

16. Bob: But you didn't say that their jobs are safe, we noticed. There'll be real trouble when this gets out! I'd look for another job now, Dot, if I were you!

17. Chair: That's the very thing we want to avoid – there'll be proper compensation in another suitable job.

18. James: Just a minute, I've been listening here carefully and am getting increasingly frustrated. If we don't keep up with technology, our competitors will overtake us – and we know what that means. Only last week that company on the other side of the city closed down; they couldn't compete – and our main competitors are breathing down our necks! That'll be our destiny, unless…

19. Chair: Well said, James, you are quite right! Look, maybe it was hopeful for us to fit all this briefing into just half an hour – let's agree to meet again and finish the discussion. Before we part, I'm handing out our brief on our opening hours over the next Bank Holiday. We want a skeleton staff to keep the depot open. Please give the sheets to your managers – tell them I'd like them back within two days.

(*Sidney now closes the meeting, crossly, and leaves the room. Bob, Ahmed and Jack remain in a huddle with the words 'industrial action' mentioned loudly; Noel sets up a practical demonstration of the POT with James; and Jasmine and April are heard consoling Dot on her speculation that she might lose her job (with an unemployed husband and three young children).*)

ANALYSING BEHAVIOUR

You can use the following list of behaviours – neutral, positive and negative – to analyse the conduct of people in a negotiation (using the abbreviation alongside each type of behaviour.)

Neutral behaviours

- **Giving information** GI
- **Trial proposal** TP
- **Disagreeing** Dis

- **Summarizing**   Sum
- **Open**   O
- **Seeking information**   SI

Positive behaviours

- **Building** on others' ideas   BU
- **Supporting** other people's ideas and proposals   Sup
- **Testing understanding** (clarifying helps to avoid misunderstandings)   TU
- **Presenting** information **assertively**   Pr
- **Signalling** that it is time to move the discussion forward   Sig
- Forming and using **proposals** to progress the meeting   Prop

Negative behaviours

- **Counter-proposals** (unless your sector of business is known for haggling, in which case this will be a valued skill)   CP
- **Defence/attack** (which can lead to 'tit-for-tat' exchanges that spiral out of control)   D/A
- **Blocking** and stating difficulties (which can generate significant frustration in opponents and reduce the wish to be supportive with more generous offers)   Bl
- Accepting inadequacy or fault (this is not about appearing to be 'perfect' but just not committing **'own goals'** in front of your opponents)   OG
- **Shutting other people out** (usually by talking too much, ignoring other people's interactions or becoming 'deaf')   SO

⏀⏀ COACHING SESSION 74

Analysing the staff meeting

Analyse the participants' behaviours at the BuGS staff meeting, using the abbreviations given above (bearing in mind that there will normally be one behaviour per sentence).

1. Which behaviour(s) seem to be overused and how might the participants have used their time more effectively?

_____

_____

_____

_____

_____

_____

_____

_____

_____

_____

_____

_____

_____

2. Draft three recommendations you would make to Sidney for chairing a more effective meeting next time.

a) _____

_____

b) _____

_____

c) _____

_____

 ONLINE RESOURCE

Analysing the staff meeting

For a commentary on this coaching session, refer to the online resources for this chapter. Go to:

www.TYCoachbooks.com/Negotiation

CONFLICT AND NEGOTIATION

Negotiation, in itself, is not really about conflict – it exists to provide an excellent way of resolving conflict. However, negotiation can also become the cause of conflict if the processes used in previous meetings have led to misunderstandings or a serious 'lose' by one of the parties. The principle of the playground fight (where the combatants are thinking 'You did that to me, so here's something back for you to think about!') *can* be replicated in adult 'battles' between:

- managers and trade union officials
- buyers and sellers
- agents and designers
- governments and civilians

and many other instances that become widely reported – sometimes from the courtroom! Whole manuals are readily available to offer resolution of disputes – with the underlying purpose of helping people *avoid* disputes and all the disruption they can cause.

Even with the best will in the world, we make errors: crises occur and pressure is brought to bear, blame is apportioned and action (sometimes disproportionate action) follows. Space doesn't allow for a full analysis of disputes here, so our focus is on the negotiating meetings themselves – and what to do if conflict does break out.

THE CAUSES OF CONFLICT

Disputes and conflict waste time and money and leave scars that may take decades to heal. It is therefore vital to make sure that we are not the cause of them. The starting position should always be the same – in negotiation terms, conflict and disputes are indicators of failure of some kind. For a variety of reasons (not least the effect on the reputation of the organizations concerned and their executives), they need to be sorted out – using the negotiation skills of the key people involved.

This table illustrates the base motivations that can lie beneath a dispute:

Motives	Outcomes
Greed	Competitiveness
Lack of trust	Exaggeration of 'facts'
Sense of injustice	Economy with the truth
Envy	Creation of enemies
Desperation	Lies

It may be rare for absolutely every phrase, punctuation mark and words/figures to be examined precisely in every contract or agreement (even when individuals are being paid to do this). Your author was alarmed and unimpressed when a lawyer once discarded a large number of pages of a property leasehold agreement with the words, 'Oh, yes! Standard stuff!' What allows people to do such a thing? Is it experience, superior knowledge or having professional indemnity insurance? Or could it be **trust**?

We hear much about the importance of 'good faith' as a vital quality in building trust between contacts – in business, social organizations and, yes, even families! And we also recognize that some people have a very economical level of good faith in their make-up and so trust does not seem to figure in their list of priorities.

 COACH'S TIP

Build trust

Trust and the development of goodwill are surely vital qualities in any relationship. Negotiation is fundamentally about trust, and breaches of trust or good faith can cause serious problems that may extend for decades.

Not a zero-sum game

In negotiation, we all want to 'win' but, in most situations, negotiation is not a zero-sum game. In other words, we exchange 'something' for 'something' and those items can be divided or amplified. When a product or service is unique, it can be difficult for a flexible outcome to be agreed and there is an application of win/lose (this can be witnessed best in an auction): 'Winners triumph, losers are disappointed and the money-exchange budget determines the outcome.' In such situations there is rarely much scope for debate, flexibility of style or persuasion, and there may not be an opportunity for a win/win deal, or it can only be achieved with great difficulty..

We must also allow for the breakdown in relations between people – caused, to some extent, by some of the factors above – but also by personal factors such as:

- personal dislike
- self-importance
- prejudice
- hatred
- desire for revenge.

It also needs to be noted that there *are* **just causes** that, without public action, would not be rectified.

⟨⟩⟨⟩ COACHING SESSION 75

How's your integrity?

If your job were on the edge of being declared redundant in a depressed market, would you be tempted to bend the truth if that enabled you to 'leapfrog' to the top of the organization's league table (making your job secure)?

1. Would you prefer to be in 'fight' or 'flight' mode in this situation? Why is this?

_____

_____

2. What other actions might you want to take?

_____

_____

_____

_____

_____

If your family were threatened by hunger or disease, would you be tempted to bribe an official if it brought security and full stomachs for your children?

3. Would you prefer to be in 'fight' or 'flight' mode in this situation? Why is this?

_____

_____

4. What other actions might you want to take?

_____

_____

_____

_____

If you felt that your 'opponent' would be offended if you refused his/her extremely generous hospitality and your company might suffer as a result, would you still feel able to insist on a black coffee and a sandwich, or would you be tempted to an 'executive lunch'?

5. Would you prefer to be in 'fight' or 'flight' mode in this situation? Why is this?

_____

_____

6. What other actions might you want to take?

_____

_____

_____

_____

_____

_____

'Reality is different', you may say. The challenges in the real world are, indeed, often bigger and even more costly – and no one much wants to know in detail what is involved until it all goes wrong (and then many supporters 'disappear' at this point). While this chapter touches on issues that you may not have to handle, it is important for all negotiators to be alert to motives that lie behind behaviours that may be witnessed in negotiations – especially the major ones.

A personal 'creed' of ethics is important or the whole world of dealing may become compromised. For example, a highly attractive offer of a large supply of 'prepacked corrugated sheeting' turns out, on delivery, to be made of corrugated cardboard rather than the expected steel. This kind of experience often occurs in some parts of the world. Maybe one or the other party is expressing greed – often at the expense of others, who are determined not to be used in this way. And tracking down the guilty parties may take years.

SOURCES OF CONFLICT

Day-to-day business activity is directed and undertaken by people. Unfortunately it also has to be recognized that people are most commonly the cause (or originators!) of disputes – and negotiation is the tool that we have to try to resolve the problems.

We have seen that negotiators may fall into two camps – those whose nature it is to be either competitive or collaborative. The following table shows the typical behaviours for each.

Competitive style	Collaborative style
Dominating	Interactive
Adversarial	Partnering
Demanding	Compromising
Inflexible	Flexible
Emotional	Rational
Evasive	Trusting/shares information
With preconceived strategy	Mutual problem solving

You will probably identify with one or other of these two styles – but neither will be 100-per-cent applicable in every situation (e.g. the competitive style may be much more appropriate in an emergency situation, while the collaborative/partnering style will bring greater benefits when long-term relationships are under scrutiny).

Apart from our 'nature', as humans we may be tempted to engage in 'games', which can also contribute to stoking up conflict. Consider the following list of conflict sources:

■ **Enjoyment**

Some people just love the idea of a row: the opportunity to prove themselves; two young 'stags' who are determined to fight the issues out until one party is exhausted (or 'mortally wounded'). Managers who know their teams well can normally predict this kind of behaviour and they will also know how best to avoid trials of strength with their team members. Commercial negotiation may be less predictable; the way hierarchies place expectations upon their management structures can cause grim determination rather than enjoyment. Either way, careful preparation and consideration of different routes must precede meetings and an analysis of the possible outcomes of failure to resolve the issues must be carried out thoroughly. In such situations, negotiators may find themselves confronted by the challenge of concluding an internal negotiation with the objective of preparing a strategy for the project.

■ **Brinkmanship**

Unfortunately, the failure of any of the parties to prepare properly (and analyse the politics of a dispute as well as the facts) may simply create a determination to push the issues right to the brink of a major conflict. Determination to keep fighting becomes greater than any perceived advantages to be gained from resolving the conflict. Unfortunately, the players can lose sight of what is a realistic goal – one that is attainable in reality. This can sometimes lead to complete reversals of win/lose deals; a macho player manipulates a contractor into believing that they cannot afford not to win the contract and finally obtains a very one-sided deal, only to have the contractor liquidate when it is too late to have another party take over the contract and still achieve that publicly quoted opening date.

▪ False expectations

Inexperienced negotiators may be lured into believing that they can obtain deals well below (or above) market price after hearing in a bar somewhere of another party's conquests. This might lead them to hold out for unrealistic deals, which may only be attainable against some hidden agenda of motives on the other side. In most disputes, 'right' is rarely totally on one side or the other and, even when it is, obtaining a declaration to that effect may not resolve the problem. Resorting to warfare, for example, may satisfy the 'hawks' in a dispute but, long after casualties have been incurred on both sides, someone has to build a vision of a just peace that the combatants can live with. Alternatives to this lead to yet more dangerous and costly disputes in the future (it is one thing to declare war and quite another to get it put 'back in the peace box with the lid screwed down tightly'.)

▪ Irritating habits

Try as we might, there may be occasions when we are unable to stop becoming irritated with an opponent, even for some quite inoffensive reason (such as ending every utterance with 'D'you know what I mean?' or sniffing all the way through the meeting). Whatever it is, we long to be able to shout 'For goodness' sake, blow your nose!' or similar. Since that might appear rude, we probably suffer in silence but, when the person then seeks a better-than-average deal as a favour, our instinct is to dismiss the request in a deliberate and final way. (If you feel that you are unable to negotiate better-than-average deals with a few favours thrown in, ask a close friend, partner or relative to give you a little feedback on any typical habit of yours that they might find irritating!)

▪ Manipulation

Some people resist any idea of negotiating – preferring a concrete arrangement that they trust is available to all. This is not the real world, but clearly some people strongly resist the idea that they might have to manipulate the facts or an application in order to obtain better terms for a deal. A practised negotiator needs to be sensitive to such a situation or lose a perfectly acceptable deal as a result of undue haste and unnecessary pressure (or manipulation, as the opponent may see it).

 COACH'S TIP

Count the cost of a conflict

For matters of principle, parties may risk life, limb, reputations and, perhaps, substantial amounts of money to be proved 'right'. The costs of resolving a conflict – before it comes to a head – may turn out to be a great deal less than the costs of a fight.

DEADLOCK AND CONFLICT

Two senior negotiators, when called upon to negotiate a team exercise, found themselves unable to reach agreement on the values they placed on the various techniques they used. The whole debate ultimately faltered on the rule 'Avoid deadlock at all costs!'

One party felt that, in his industry, it was totally unrealistic to 'throw 50-pound notes at the situation just to avoid deadlock'. The other emphasized that, in her experience, 'time is money' and that, while she could conceive of situations where stalemates could occur, deadlock simply protracted negotiation and increased the attendant costs – a definite no-no in her highly profitable enterprise. (This pragmatic approach should be remembered, of course, when matters of principle are involved: is it better to take 'the hit' now and get on with the next deal than to waste time arguing about this one?)

Identifying the issues which may become deal-busters are important in any negotiation. This step should be an integral part of the Discussion and Proposal phases. The reluctance of the opponent to move on a particular issue – even when concessions or inducements are offered – may cause the spectre of a 'no deal' stalemate to arise.

○○ COACHING SESSION 76

Resolving a deadlock

1. If you have been involved in a deadlock, how did you resolve it?

_____

_____

_____

_____

_____

_____

_____

2. If the situation resolved itself, how did this happen?

_____

_____

_____

3. What would you do differently in the future?

_____

_____

_____

_____

_____

_____

THE POLITICS OF NEGOTIATION

As we have seen, different people see negotiation in quite different ways and we need to look for the politics behind the other party's actions. Broadly speaking, the more competitive they are at heart, the more likely they will be to adopt a competitive approach to a negotiation.

For instance, they may see the process as akin to any of the following:

- **A 'race'**

Only the winner will walk away with the gold medal and everything else is second best (often described as a zero-sum game).

- **Point-scoring**

An event in which the other party may be weakened by constant point-scoring is mainly done to impress an audience (usually their own side).

- **Bidding**

Bidding (as at an auction) is a process in which one 'customer' is manipulated to believe that he or she is bidding for a deal against other unseen players.

- **Haggling**

This is a form of bartering just as if the product or service is being traded in a street market.

- **Gaining market share**

Pressure to win to protect or gain market share or benefits for the consumer is a method that drives many commercial bargains and it can lead to over-preoccupation with price issues; the risk is that many other valuable goals are overlooked.

- **'Arm-wrestling'**

This is an opportunity to boost one's ego by exhibiting power and strength – the principal aim being the subjugation of the opponent.

Conflict resolution methods

The processes used by negotiators to resolve differences may also give an insight into their view of conflict. For example, some parties may be quick to resort to:

- **Law**

This is where the 'best' (most expensive?) lawyer may stand a better chance of winning, leaving the opponent with a very public, and expensive, 'loser' status.

- **Arbitration**

Where the negotiator is convinced of the rightness of his or her case, they will see the process of arbitration as the means of achieving the goal.

- **Pressure groups**

Resorting to the media may buttress the case being pressed by a negotiator – for example, Greenpeace is able to generate considerable sympathy among non-members for particular ecological actions and fight a case for the wider public good (even though their committed support may appear to be small in paid-up numbers). Its engagement of the media may bring about achievement of its objectives even when it is in a 'David and Goliath' struggle.

- **Taking 'hostages'**

This could include a unilateral decision to cut off communities with the withdrawal of transport services or perhaps the decision to build a bridge to replace a ferry, the cost of which has to be paid for with expensive toll fees. Negotiators will seek ways of ensuring that the aggressors in such cases do not benefit from their actions.

- **The 'honest broker'**

The party may seek a reputable body to act as mediator in the case of a struggle; the higher the perceived standing of the broker, the more likely the parties will be to present objective evidence, agree procedures and debate the issues.

COACHING SESSION 77

Discovering the 'politics'

Resolution of the issues listed above should, ideally be swift and economical so that the disruption is only short term and not too draining on what should be productive activity.

1. Do any of the above approaches match your experience? Note them here.

_____

_____

_____

_____

2. How did you resolve these challenging situations?

_____

_____

_____

_____

_____

MOTIVATORS OF CONFLICT

Apart from the style factors considered above, conflict may be motivated by fear, blackmail, or a sense of unfairness (misplaced or otherwise). You may have witnessed some or all of the following:

■ **Defeat or humiliation**

Negotiators or parties may feel obliged to fight simply because they feel they have no option; they have been boxed in and the alternative to fighting is to accept conditions which will be perceived as a humiliating defeat. (This position can also lead to a damaging lose/lose, where the pressurized party reclaims 'ownership of the ball and refuses to allow the game to continue'.)

■ **Retaliation**

'You did that to me, so I am doing this to you!' We might describe this as playground politics, as such tit-for-tat tactics can get out of hand.

■ **Thin end of the wedge**

Where one party senses that pressure from the opponent could quickly lead to a trend, they may feel more obliged to steel themselves for a battle to dissuade other similar proposals being advanced.

■ **Fear**

Many high-profile disputes are kept in balance by both parties, who fear that their opponents may adopt similar tactics, with possible detrimental and unpredictable effects. This is sufficient to stop the use of that particular tactic.

■ **Test of strength**

Sometimes a conflict might be a test of strength or willingness to fight set up by a surrogate body designed to expose the main party's tactics. For example, in international relations, the Cuban Missile Crisis might be seen as the USSR's testing of the United States' resolve to prevent an expansion of nuclear potential on its own doorstep. ('Cuba today, where tomorrow?')

■ **Macho power**

Large is reckoned by most people to mean powerful, but how can this be demonstrated? An obvious way is by bullying other, smaller players in the market – competitors or even clients. So a very large retailer might deliberately breach pricing protocols (e.g. recommended retail prices) as a competitive weapon, but also to flex its muscles on a much wider stage.

■ **Guerrilla warfare**

In some forums, the desire to be destructive is much stronger than the desire to be constructive. This may not necessarily be an expression of hatred – just that the players dislike the system so much that they are determined to change it for good.

■ **Levers**

These can provide highly effective means of obtaining a resolution of disputes, especially when one party is desperate to get on with, say, a major project. For example, a company anxious to establish a new bipartisan forum for health and safety procedures covering its national operations may find itself held up by one of its employee representatives who is urgently seeking major change in one small, local plant.

With this collection of motivators, it should also be remembered that conflict is often stoked up by many observers, players, the media, and even individual citizens. Politicians sometimes find themselves looking over their shoulders and considering what public opinion makes of a particular issue before becoming committed to a positive course of action. This concern can sometimes motivate the behaviour of senior managers, too – in commercial markets as well as in industrial relations disputes. Many a 'macho' manager – regularly using expletives to describe what he (or she) intends to do to an opponent – turns out to 'purr like a pussy cat' in the privacy of the opponent's office.

COACHING SESSION 78

Seeing through conflict behaviour

Such behaviour is intended to create an effect on the 'troops' but rarely cuts much ice once the individual's cover is blown. However, until this day arrives, perhaps all less experienced negotiators reporting to such a 'macho' manager might model themselves on this type of behaviour.

What do you think could be the consequences of this type of behaviour? Note down your thoughts here.

_____

_____

_____

_____

_____

With patience and care, it should be possible to avoid a conflict situation arising in the first place. If conflict does arise, the 'Best Alternative to a Negotiated Settlement' (BATNeS) may hardly seem to present a desirable way out. Resorting to force (or the lawyers) may not be very attractive either (just think of the delays and the legal costs!), so conflict resolution needs to be given careful consideration.

DEFUSING CONFLICT

Here are some ways of defusing conflict in negotiation meetings with the objective of achieving consensus and a win/win deal:

- Ignoring the conflict by focusing on objectives
- Smoothing things over
- Withdrawal of one (or both) of the parties
- Resolution by working it through
- Arbitration by a third party

Focusing on objectives

As we have seen, conflicting behaviour and attitudes in meetings can provide effective distractions from the main business in hand. Clearly, this is unhelpful; it might be thought of as 'fun' – or even tactical – to provoke an opponent but this may turn out to be a wasteful game if it results in deadlock. Both sides need to meet the objectives of the meeting (unless one party has a clear intention to achieve a lose/lose result, in which case it should have been identified in their opponent's preparation).

Smoothing things over

Diplomats are past masters at smoothing over difficulties. All their years of training have helped them smooth over even aggressive situations as 'little local difficulties' and, even when their 'masters' have fallen out, they try to maintain the closest of relationships with their opposite numbers at the local level. This is what they are paid to do and, more often than not, it works.

Conciliation services try to focus on the same role. For example, the marriage guidance counsellor may try to help the parties to express, and then resolve, their disputes and difficulties by smoothing out the emotions and aggression in favour of the greater objective. A highly skilled diplomat or conciliator will often be able to turn conflict and disagreement into agreement all round.

Withdrawal

Once the full impact of the possibilities resulting from deadlock or conflict become clear, one of the parties may draw back from their position – enabling some further exchange of concessions. This will work well where they can be convinced that their opponent will not simply move on to a further demand. In other words, recognition of the 'greater good' – or larger issues may motivate the parties to sink their differences.

Withdrawal of one party (by recess) may allow for a period of reflection on both sides. Trying to be objective about the situation may still defeat highly emotional negotiators and in this instance the only way to make progress would be to replace the negotiators themselves.

Resolution

Conflict resolution is not always a pretty sight! Macho negotiators have been known to threaten opponents in meetings with intimidating behaviour (e.g. rolling up sleeves in a threatening way) and, sadly, it is not unknown for such situations to lead to a punch-up in some back alley. Managers can be just as guilty and, while fisticuffs may be the ultimate in aggressive behaviour, some people find a really good row very satisfying. Expressing feelings in an unrestrained way (what politicians might call a 'robust discussion') at least lets all the parties know where they stand.

The dangers are obvious. In the general melee, things may be said for which there can be no easy apology and bruised egos simply result in an increasing determination that the opponents will not be allowed to succeed. Once again, commitment to ultimate agreement needs to be paramount to make such tactics successful.

Arbitration

In the precise sense of the word, an arbitrator could be described as a go-between – a counsellor who seeks to advise both parties on their dispute, encourage objective thought and suggest solutions that will suit both sides. Sometimes the arbiter is needed because the two sides have completely lost control of a negotiation and cannot bear even to share the same room as the other party. So the conciliator becomes the mouthpiece or 'conduit' for the two sides.

The arbitration process goes further than this because both sides (or all parties) must guarantee that they will agree to its decisions. There is no point in going to arbitration unless the parties are prepared to implement the decisions of the arbiter, whatever they may be. Arbitration is not an automatic method of resolving conflict unless the parties agree to this in advance and, ideally, there should be some legal framework or sanctions that will apply if the final settlement is not supported.

BEHAVIOURS TO AVOID

Skilled and experienced negotiators try to avoid manipulating their opponents if they believe that this will lead to conflict – and to a lose/lose result.

Specific behaviours to be avoided at this point are:

- **counter-proposals** – deliberately adopting a haggling style

- **irritators** – where one party deliberately uses verbal, or non-verbal, behaviour to provoke their opponent(s), which may result in an emotional outburst. This means that the instigators of the irritants can grasp the high moral ground by making it seem that they are the responsible, reliable, emotionally mature players who have the real interests of the company/state/union/manufacturing plant at heart.

- **argument dilution** – an 'own goal' created by mixing sound and weak arguments in support of a case. The mistake lies in listing all these points together so that the opponent may choose a weak one to discredit, followed by another, and then another. Any sound arguments will be lost within this belittling process, creating a 'moral victory' (because all the other issues proved to be worthless).

- **defence and attack spirals** – these provoke playground warfare which can easily get out of hand. Little is gained by an irrational discussion, let alone an absolute row. There is probably no jury to convince, no judge or procedure to keep things on track – only a fast-declining prospect of persuading the opposition to reach agreement. Skilled negotiators do all they can to ignore and avoid reacting to emotional behaviour.

- **blocking** – objecting to proposals without supporting reasons can be annoying in the extreme and contribute to the creation of a conflict. Sweet reason is the rock on which logical debate is founded and negotiation will be much more likely to fail when reason is absent.

COACH'S TIP

Ignore weak arguments

When an opponent has fallen into the trap of argument dilution (perhaps through naiveté), try to avoid creating negative reactions by focusing on the weak arguments to demolish them. Given the probability that this behaviour indicates inexperience, the skilled negotiator will not worry about addressing the weak arguments but simply address the one or two strong ones.

COACHING SESSION 79

Behaviour analysis

Rate how often you use the techniques described above. Fill in the following table.

Technique	Never	Sometimes	Often	Always
Haggling/ counter-proposals				
Irritators				
Argument dilution				

Defence/attack spirals				
Blocking				

'Sometimes' is an allowable standard – but anything more means that you are probably contributing to your own problems by stirring up your opponents. Try out a more reasoning style in negotiations in your domestic life and, when you can see some positive results, try to adapt the method in your business world.

 COACH'S TIP

Keep your cool

If an attack spirals out of control and leads to verbal abuse, take a mental side-step and allow the 'arrows' to fly over your shoulder, keeping cool and showing that you have no intention to join in their 'game'. Counting to ten before responding may be a valuable way of thinking before acting – or speaking, if the hurt of an unjust accusation or downright lie is too much to ignore. A recess will help to calm emotions and tempers.

Psychological pressures and games

These can also contribute to emotional situations, deadlock and even conflict and are not normally used by skilled negotiators. Such pressures include the following:

- **Taking the higher seat** (while the opponent has the lower one)
- Deliberately **facing the opponent into the light** so that he/she finds it difficult to focus on facial expression and eye contact
- Adopting a **low reactor style of interaction** (i.e. deliberately not saying very much), which can be intimidating, especially for a natural extrovert (naive extroverts may not even notice this happening)

- Imposing a completely **unrealistic timescale** on the meeting and then calling 'time-out' before the opponent has had a chance to present their case – throwing serious doubts on the party's intentions to reach anything other than an imposed solution

- Doing everything possible to **shut out** the opponent (perhaps by over-talking or constantly interrupting).

You will doubtless be able to recall opponents who have tried some of these tactics, and you may have even tried some of them yourself. There is little doubt that, if used in subtle ways, they can be made to work. However, if they are unsubtle, they are likely simply to attract ridicule and put you at a severe disadvantage.

Blaming others

There is a risk that, unchecked – and without considerable effort to prevent escalation – conflict can take the progressive form illustrated in the following diagram:

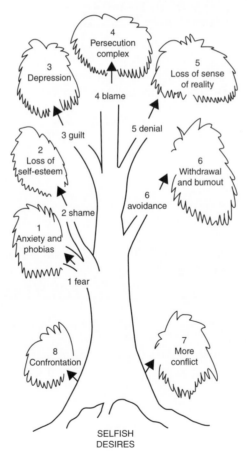

The roots, shoots and offshoots of conflict (after David Cormack, 1989)

The negotiation process can boost over-confidence in some people and it is easy for their self-belief system to blame others when debates fail to reach agreement. Negotiators do need to bear in mind the possibility of a lose/lose outcome if conflict situations have not been resolved through discussion and problem-solving. Regardless of how improbable it might seem, negotiators always have choices – even if the only option is not to go ahead at all.

TOWARDS A BETTER DEAL

As we have seen, conflict can be a natural element in negotiations – especially when the parties feel that they are in competitive situations. The obvious way to avoid this is for both parties to try to focus on the big issues and the overall objectives, and avoid precipitate action or behaviour that may simply provoke a conflict.

COACHING SESSION 80

Dispute resolution

1. What experiences (first- or second-hand) have you had of taking a dispute to a third party and gaining endorsement of your position?

_____

_____

_____

_____

2. What advice would you give new entrants to negotiating so that their authority or bargaining position is not jeopardized?

_____

_____

_____

_____

_____

COACH'S TIP

Focus on the goals

Focusing on the goals to be achieved – and the benefits to be gained – may help to restore a level of motivation and intention to reach agreement where these factors have been eroded. Commitment to ultimate agreement needs to be paramount to make all other tactics successful.

COACHING SESSION 81

Assessing your skills

Avoiding distractions and focusing on your main objectives is the most important way to prevent a conflict situation arising. Answering the following questions honestly will help you assess your skills and abilities in this area.

1. In your experience, what distractions are most likely to sidetrack you from your main objectives?

_____

_____

_____

_____

2. How could you use a checklist or notes to keep yourself on track in future?

_____

_____

_____

_____

3. How could working with a partner help?

_____

_____

_____

_____

_____

4. How would you keep your self-control and maintain a friendly conversation, even with opponents who have acted irresponsibly or provocatively?

_____

_____

_____

_____

5. How would you create a recess without it appearing that you are under pressure?

_____

_____

_____

_____

6. What key pieces of advice would you pass on to a new entrant to negotiating?

_____

_____

_____

_____

_____

Revealing feelings

A very powerful tactic – but one that should not be overused for fear of it losing its effect – is the sharing or revealing of inner feelings. If negotiation is about persuading other parties to move towards the position you desire, such a result is hardly likely if they are feeling angry, upset or frustrated with you or your organization.

A 'poker face' and masterly self-control may conceal your feelings most of the time and so revealing them in a simple sentence can have a powerful effect. Understatement will usually have more impact than an emotional outburst, however. Having cleared the air, the players will be able to focus on the ultimate goal: a deal freely entered into that benefits both sides and can be readily implemented.

Rebuilding trust

When all else fails, discreet enquiries around the market may reveal the extent of conflict elsewhere. If it looks as if you are the only individual or organization to suffer these problems, perhaps you should ask yourself how you can rebuild trust and restore your reputation. You may need to enter into a new round of negotiations to re-establish the status quo and rebuild your reputation for integrity. (Alternatively, it might be time to find another role!) Either way, revising the whole process from the beginning will not come amiss.

COACHING SESSION 82

Implementing an agreement

Check the following points to see whether the agreement you reached was the best one possible. Add a tick or a cross as appropriate.

1. Have I ensured that both/all parties are in accord with exactly what has been agreed? ☐

2. Have I written to confirm the above situation? ☐

3. Am I aware of whom I must contact to put the proposal into effect? ☐

4. Have I prioritized my activities to ensure that all time contracts will be achieved? ☐

5. Have I established the check controls I must implement to ensure that the agreement is carried out? ☐

6. We won the contract but was it really the winning deal we were seeking? ☐

7. Did it really meet all the other parties' aspirations? ☐

8. Now that the deal is done, were our 'what-ifs' plausible? ☐

9. Could any of them still threaten the implementation? ☐

10. Do we have a contingency plan if this should happen? ☐

Now answer the following questions.

1. Looking back, what we have learned from this negotiation and contract?

_____

_____

_____

_____

_____

2. How could it have been improved?

_____

_____

_____

_____

Add any action points to your action plan and make notes on how you could make improvements next time.

Ultimately, project management techniques help negotiators avoid many of the difficulties described above. Perhaps this is a further development area for you? Skilled negotiators are people who have a track record of significant success with no implementation failures. Your aim should be to achieve this status and reputation!

To recap, these are the behaviours that mark out skilled negotiators:

- Making proposals and not counter-proposals!

- Building behaviour to add to or change an opponent's proposals (making it appear that it was their idea all along)

- Seeking information by asking open questions (rather than creating a 'fog' with myriad facts and too much information and opinion)

- Active listening (giving nods and maintaining eye contact to demonstrate interest in hearing the other party's views)

- Showing empathy (to demonstrate understanding of the other party's feelings)

- Clarifying behaviours (especially through testing their understanding of what has been said, and summarizing)

- Giving support/agreement, where possible, and praising offers and welcoming ideas (which helps to generate more of them)

- Labelling behaviour before it is used (e.g. 'May I just ask a question?' helps to gain the other party's attention)
- Bringing others into the discussion (e.g. 'I am sure you have some views on that idea.')
- Pausing to let them respond
- Sharing inner feelings (used sparingly, or it loses its effect).

THE PROD-ProSC MAP

Stage	Issues
P = Prepare	
a) People	Who am I meeting? With what authority?
	Who else is likely to be present?
	What do I know about the culture and style of representatives of this business?
b) Place	Where will we meet? Home or away?
	What is the meeting room like?
	How can I make the communications work for me?
	How affected am I likely to be by the personal comfort factors?
R = Research	What do we know about the trend of deals in this sector? How might this affect our goals?
	Have I a clear shopping list of objectives and parameters worked out for each one?
	What could be our opponents' position?
	How could I find out in advance?
	Who might have the power in this relationship?
	How could it be used for mutual benefit?

Stage	Issues
O = Open	How should I open the meeting? What ice-breaking topics might be used? Are there any probing questions I could ask? How could we establish some common ground?
D = Debate and discuss	What style of conversation should I adopt? Collaborative/consensual/competitive? What kind of response is this likely to bring?
Pro = Propose **Conflict management**	How will I resist the temptation to move too quickly/slowly? How could trial proposals help? How will I ensure that my proposals are conditional? **What if we disagree in a major way?** **How could we resolve the conflict?**
S = Summarize	How good am I at using summaries in meetings? How will I remember to use summaries during and at the end of the meeting?
C = Close	Who will be responsible for tracking progress at the meeting and at the end? How can I ensure that appropriate notes are taken and that they are accurate and complete? How strong is my decision-making ability? What methods of closing can I use most effectively? If my authority is challenged, how will I manage this?

Once you have explored your current stage, note in your action plan any areas that might need more attention.

 **NEXT STEPS**

Conflict can be a natural element of negotiations, especially when the parties feel they are in competitive situations. The obvious solution is for both parties to try to focus on the big issues and the overall objectives – and avoid precipitate action or behaviour that may provoke a dispute.

The next chapter is about summarizing and closing the meeting. You will learn the importance of signalling agreement and using summaries as progress commentaries. You will also find out how to handle hesitation and reluctance, how to maintain momentum, and how to spot the behaviour and attitudes that will help or hinder agreement.

TAKEAWAYS

You should now have a full understanding of how conflict can arise (or be generated) through motives and actions, before, during and after a negotiation.

When have you experienced conflict arising before a negotiation?

_____

_____

_____

_____

_____

_____

How did you cope with it?

_____

_____

_____

_____

_____

_____

What additional actions could you have taken (now that you have completed this chapter)?

_____

_____

_____

_____

_____

_____

During a negotiation, how will you respond to conflict should it arise?

What methods of defusing conflict might you use?

Which of your habitual behaviours could generate conflict and are therefore to be avoided?

What will be your main aim, if an acceptable deal should be threatened?

After the negotiation, how will you ensure that the trust that has been built will be maintained?

_____

_____

_____

_____

_____

How will you ensure that there is no lasting damage to a continuing relationship?

_____

_____

_____

_____

What further action (if any) may help to restore the relationship in the long term?

_____

_____

_____

_____

_____

SUMMARIZING AND CLOSING

- Understand the importance of signalling agreement.
- Use summaries as progress commentaries.
- Label, listen and handle hesitation and reluctance.
- Cope with human factors in maintaining momentum.
- Progress summaries towards the close.
- Spot the behaviour and attitudes that will help or hinder agreement.

In terms of the PROD-ProSC model that we have been following, this chapter is about the S part: the summarizing and concluding sections of the negotiation. It links together the following issues and concerns:

- How do I plan to summarize?
- What needs to be bolted down?
- How can we avoid implementation failure?
- What kind of written record do we need?

When all is said and done, what the negotiator needs as an outcome from a negotiation discussion is simply something like: 'I agree', 'That's fine', 'Let's do it', or even 'Yes'. However, some people make these noises of agreement and then, with the next breath, they start to back-pedal, try to impose new or additional conditions, or add in some extra requirement – with no review of costs, price or timing – as a consequence. If the earlier stages had been built on an atmosphere of conditional bargaining (seemingly in balance), acceptance of the latest condition could threaten to push the deal into a win/lose – where they win and you lose.

People try to do these kinds of things if they think they can get away with it, but the costs can be high. Of course, you could roll back the meeting to stage one and begin all over again – but can you afford the time? This kind of tactic is often chosen just before a deadline for tenders, when open-market tendering must be closed and your target period (when your objectives are re-appraised, monitored and rewarded) is about to end. Perhaps the client knew about this timing because the supplier's representative joked about it over a social drink…

One unpleasant tactic is the threat to put off a decision that could cost the supplier dearly, especially if bonuses are calculated on new business that is contracted. People do this kind of thing if it will earn them more concessions, but would you want to renegotiate a contract if it is going to affect your performance review? The moral is to be very cautious when answering questions about relations between contracted business and bonuses.

PROGRESSING TOWARDS THE CLOSE

As the debate process inches towards agreement, there tend to be many opportunities for those involved to reflect on and review the formal deal – and to think about the pros and cons of the arrangements discussed. At this stage we need to understand the normal hesitations that affect negotiators. Concerns may take the form of various questions:

- Have we a clear idea of the benefits this deal will provide?

- How sure are we that the specification matches our needs?

- How reliable are any quoted features and benefits?

- How certain are we that this supplier will support us should any feature not materialize?

The concerns on the other side of the table would not be very different:

- Is this a reliable client with a commitment to adopt a project/scheme like ours?

- Do they have broad commitment from senior management?

- Does this client have a financial track record with our company?

- If not, what credit check/budget check can be carried out to ascertain their liquidity?

Staff relations

In the staff relations field, such discussions are sometimes held under a threat of official or unofficial staff action (e.g. a ban on overtime), which can focus everyone's attention on the 'losers' from implementation of a new scheme – rather than the positive advantages. Changes that could have a positive effect on improving productivity may prove highly disruptive before it is even proved that such changes will increase the company's profits.

As a matter of principle, most businesses would find it unacceptable to be facing negotiations with a background threat of industrial action. Peace and better understanding of the impacts of change would most likely have to be added to the agenda for any substantial changes to be accepted on to joint staff/management discussions. Given the way the hypothetical discussion has developed, a new plan is likely to be needed to guide both management and staff representatives.

SUMMARIES AS 'PROGRESS COMMENTARIES'

Top negotiators use summaries to confirm areas of agreement as they work through meetings with clients or suppliers. This is vital as a way of clarifying the practicalities of 'Who is going to do what for whom, and when?' These actions need full understanding and commitment, without which there is likely to have to be a new subset of conversations (and possibly negotiations). Matters that were unforeseen but now come to light can threaten to derail the implementation of the agreement – and anyone who has had that experience would never want to repeat it.

Don't be surprised if this summary uncovers:

- misunderstandings

- outstanding 'loose ends'

- past allowances that need to be integrated into this deal

- organizational changes that may mean implementation could be by different people

- deadlines that may need some flexibility to allow for earlier projects running late or conditions that may affect the timing of new projects.

 COACH'S TIP

Make the meaning of the summary clear

Your detailed summary is essential if all parties are to agree – not just to what is written down but also to the *practical* meaning of the implementation of the agreement (i.e. who will do what when – and with what costs).

The contribution of summaries in meetings can offer significant advantages to all those present. Without a summary, discussion can revolve around the issues several times with either player simply repeating subjects, topics and ideas already covered in some detail. Apart from the fact that this may appear boring and repetitive (and therefore demotivate the participants), the discussion may not contribute clarity to the meeting – quite the reverse, in fact! (Frustrated negotiators have been heard complaining that such occasions can be 'like trying to wade through very sticky mud'.)

CLARIFYING THE AGREEMENT

The processes involved in a new agreement or contract can be exceptionally detailed – and every effort must be made to clarify the data so that no misunderstandings can ensue. This means that time must be invested in 'due diligence'. On the one hand, it is important to avoid generalizations that turn out to be unenforceable (for example, 'Payment will be made as soon as possible' is a worthless statement). On the other hand, too much fine detail may simply make the final contract impractical.

An agreed conciliation route/authority will be important, should an unforeseen problem arise later on (which may prove difficult to reconcile for the parties alone). How many times have we heard the following:

■ 'But I thought we/they agreed…'?

■ 'I was sure that we agreed that, but it does not seem to be in the minutes'?

■ 'You did include cancellation terms in the contract, didn't you?'?

Thorough summaries will save time and help the meeting towards its final phase. High-profile negotiators may claim that they cannot spend much time summarizing behaviour but, when used effectively, the result will pay for itself over and over again in avoiding misunderstandings and potential disputes.

COACH'S TIP

Use summaries to avoid errors

Apart from raising the spectre of misunderstanding and confusion, the absence of strategic summaries may contribute to considerable errors in the ultimate agreement – and possibly the contract or communiqué.

Signalling, labelling and listening

To ensure that your meeting progresses efficiently towards a complete and fully implementable deal, it is vital that negotiators track all exchanges (e.g. quantities versus price paid) and note down those agreements – taking care to query anything new or that appears to have changed. The signal for this process is usually the use of the simple word: 'So…'

Giving your full attention and engaging your listening skills at this point are essential, since acceptance of even a simple, short summary will be assumed to indicate that the overall agreement has been approved. Otherwise, what was the point of having a summary? Here we can visualize a main disadvantage of working with highly reactive and extrovert opponents, who prefer to speak rather than listen and think!

If any detail (no matter how small) seems to differ from your understanding of the earlier remarks/conversation, you should challenge these items before the close of the topic/debate/meeting, or the assumption could be made that agreement has been reached by exception.

Overcoming reluctance

What if your opponent finds all this checking tiresome – maybe suggesting that queries be raised *after* the agreement is signed and that caveats or codicils be attached to the contract to clarify issues later? This may be tempting, but it could lead to nightmares for your legal department (if you have one). Again, why the hurry? If a problem of interpretation in a contract arises – post-signature – this could become an expensive matter for a lawyer to disentangle.

COACH'S TIP

Check the written words

Always ensure that the written words explain unequivocally what is in your mind – and that of your fellow negotiators. This might delay the signing while the language is double-checked by your specialists.

COACHING SESSION 83

Dealing with obstructive tactics

Unfortunately, many problems can become apparent at this late stage – most likely those that have been unstated previously. Here are six not uncommon situations. What would you do about them?

1. Negotiators really want a discount and are awaiting an offer but, when one does not materialize, they fail to make a case for one – but are still holding out against accepting the deal.

_____

_____

_____

_____

2. Negotiators neglect to mention that the authorizing signatory is someone not present but who will want to question you very closely before signing the deal off.

3. Vendors neglect to mention that the scheme or product is back-ordered owing to a huge response to the latest advertising promotion.

4. There is discovery/disclosure that the supplier's factory source is suspected of abusing employees' human rights on the other side of the world.

5. Opponents deliberately mis-summarize issues that have been agreed – obviously bringing more benefit to their position than that of their opponent.

6. One party promotes false deadlines to pressurize the other to close the deal (increasingly effective if this coincides with a promotional price).

The use of these tactics could quickly create a feeling of a deliberate attempt to create obstacles that threaten to frustrate the deal. Similarly, attaching stringent legal conditions can have a similar effect and, with complicated contracts, potential contractors would be well advised to ensure that the ultimate contract agreement is capable of being implemented.

THE IMPACT OF CONVERSATIONAL STYLE

Your conversational style is likely to be under close scrutiny at this stage, too. If, for example, your normal pattern of interaction is to talk for 80 per cent of the time and listen for 20 per cent of the time, there is a risk that your opponent will feel bombarded with too much information and that their opinions go unheard. There is also a risk that people will feel that much of you say can safely be ignored. Methods of interaction tend to match our personalities and these can lead us into occupations that suit these attributes successfully. The push-style negotiator will tend to be the seller in an interaction, in opposition to the pull-style negotiator (the buyer).

The challenge is to recognize the risk of imbalance and use more self-awareness and discipline in negotiations (and this learning could be started in non-occupational conversations). Negotiators are rarely selected for their conversational abilities, with the result that power can be misused, time wasted and poor deals transacted.

COACH'S TIP

Improve through training

A very effective way of improving your conversational skills is to attend an interactive training event, which uses video role-play exercises with coach-led analysis and feedback.

COACHING SESSION 84

Practise push/pull habits

For total versatility in interactive meetings, it would be good to practise the opposite style from the one in which you are strongest. That is, if you are normally a push-style person, try practising the pull style in 'no-risk' conversations. Remember that, while doing much of the talking is a recognizable and natural push style, continual questioning can be quite alarming to some people. Your aim is to balance the two styles.

Prepare your plan here – i.e. who you might work with (and why) and some practice subjects you could use.

_____

_____

_____

_____

_____

_____

_____

THE EFFECTS OF ROLE ON CLOSING A DEAL

It might seem unnecessary to dwell on how to close a negotiation since anyone in selling has to make themselves competent at closing sales, or they are unlikely to survive in the marketing environment. It could also be argued, similarly, that buyers/procurement executives have the same understandings, simply through their natural involvement with their sales partners.

However, the negotiation role tends to be more demanding and often involves wider issues than the familiar ones of units and price. Lawyers, for example, are often involved in negotiating deals, both in and out of court, and often these involve resolving disputed contracts between sellers and buyers. Then there are the employee relations and social fields – which are regulated by legislation and codes of practice – in which failure to agree could create significant disruption, inconvenience and cost to potentially millions of people.

Where the first group of players should have considerable insights into fashion, market value and popularity, so that any mistakes in the small print can be more than compensated by the popular response of clients, the second group has a big involvement with the courts of popular opinion – especially if their negotiations have an impact on the continuing provision of public services (e.g. public transport or public hygiene).

The common ground between these job roles and disciplines is that they can all use the techniques that this book is covering to deliver excellent results. What might appear to be a limiting role in fact delivers considerable strength for any negotiator, whose behaviour will almost certainly be thorough, determined and persistent.

COACHING SESSION 85

Cementing the relationship

Concluding your negotiation session needs to be seen as just the first essential step in a new relationship brought about by the agreement.

Note down here some ways in which you can cement the relationship (and the deal). Words are good – but actions will be better!

_____

_____

_____

_____

_____

_____

_____

FINAL CLARIFICATIONS

Since the aim of this book is to help you conclude more winning deals, this section seeks to clarify how advantageous proposals can be tested and then approved for implementation. Critically, this needs to include a full test of the proposed deal – with sufficient clarity to ensure that there are no evasions, ambiguities or guesswork.

Here are some examples of successful 'lead-ins':

- 'Before we go any further, let's just clarify how this new system would work...'

- 'We need to understand how this new approach would benefit our users...'

- 'And how many of these systems would you have in use in this country...?'

- 'We would want to see this in operation – how could you arrange that...?'

An important word in each example here is 'would', which implies that further commitment is likely to depend on a successful demonstration and subsequent agreement of terms. Also, the use of 'we' (rather than 'I') gives more weight to the fact that the negotiator is authorized to commit their organization to this deal. The supplier may well want to ensure that there is a real commitment in outline – as the prospect could prove to be an expensive time-waster if no written confirmation (or order) is placed. If the supplier can satisfy concerns in some way at this point, a 'close' could swiftly follow.

👤👤 COACHING SESSION 86

Testing closing language

Concluding your negotiation session needs to be done using the right language.

Write down here the closing remarks you might use to seal a deal.

_____

_____

_____

_____

_____

_____

The pattern of questioning from the other side of the table would not be very different:

- 'Is this a reliable client with a commitment to adopt a scheme like ours?'
- 'Do they have broad commitment from senior management?'
- 'Does this client have a financial track record with our company?'
- 'If not, what credit check/budget check can be carried out to ascertain their liquidity?'

What is essential here is that trust between those involved in discussion be matched with positive criteria (e.g. a letter of intent) that the commitment from both organizations is strong enough – and the financial resources are available – for the contract to be drafted, agreed and signed. Mistakes are often made in both of these areas, resulting in expensive time-wasting.

CLOSING EXPECTATIONS

It should be a given that the meeting will involve an exchange of papers – maybe initialled to indicate agreement of the parties – with fully detailed criteria, so that there can be no misunderstandings of the data. If possible, have these papers prepared in advance to save yet another meeting or an awkward pause while they are prepared. This time may often be used as an opportunity for more informal discussion – perhaps over lunch.

Any positive result may feel like a reward for all the advance preparation and discussion, as long as it is close to the original expectations (otherwise there may not be much to celebrate). The summary of the result at this point will give both parties the chance to consider whether sufficient progress has been made to enable a final agreement to be drawn up. If this is not possible, the parties may agree simply to meet again in the future (diarized or not).

 COACH'S TIP

Beware loose talk

Beware the impact of loose talk in these closing situations, which are still critical to the eventual outcome. Talking too freely can sometimes unwittingly contribute to the unravelling of the very understanding that has just been reached.

Lack of any positive intention arising from the meeting may indicate on the part of either (or both) sides:

- a lack of intention or motivation in the first instance

- the leaching away of good intentions, before the meeting started, for some reason discussed (or experienced) in the meeting itself

- a recognition that the issues are more complicated/technical/vague/detailed than could be realistically tackled in the time allowed for the meeting.

It is often the mark of inexperienced negotiators that the most they feel able to agree is the date of a further meeting. That is not to say that either party should feel obliged to agree when they are unsure about the sense of doing this. Clearly, most negotiations take place in an environment of free will and this means that there may not be an agreement from this meeting. It is, after all, everyone's right to mull things over.

Closing the gap between discussion/proposals and the final decision may need rather more patience and persistence. Skilled negotiators know that they are not wasting time in early phases of relationship building, which will pay off when sticking points are uncovered in the final stages of discussion. Clarifying any remaining inhibitions or sticking points is essential before attempting to close the deal – especially when the implementation of the agreement is considered. After all the earlier discussion of the issues, it may be that loose ends of implementation could still turn the deal sour.

Here are some examples of loose ends:

- 'Who will be responsible for writing up this agreement?'

- 'Where and when shall we convene for a review meeting?'

- 'How will this delivery be made, and when?'

These may seem obvious points but many negotiations have come to grief through inadequate coverage of the detail – and the details often make the difference between a win/win and a lose/lose deal.

THE FINAL CLOSE

At this stage you can still use tactics to close the deal. Bargaining may be helped by:

- recognizing and dealing with any outstanding issues/obstacles

- summarizing

- seeking approval and a 'Yes!'

- offering an additional concession

- proposing a brief recess

- using the either/or technique

- threatening to pull out ('crowding' or calling time-out).

Beware of your opponent using similar blocking techniques, such as imposing deadlines, summarizing earlier areas of agreement to block new ones or to prevent a fast move from 'base' to 'final square'. This might reflect 'gamesmanship' played by a naive negotiator – risking an unpredictable outcome.

COACHING SESSION 87

How will you close?

Think about how you could project confidence, trust and reassurance as you close the deal.

1. Think about the words you could use. Write them down here:

_____

_____

_____

_____

_____

2. What body language should you use or maintain?

_____

_____

_____

_____

_____

3. What irritators should you avoid?

_____

_____

_____

_____

_____

COACHING SESSION 88

Helping and hindering progress

In any negotiation, behaviours and attitudes can help or hinder progress towards achieving agreement. Which ones have you experienced or used yourself?

Tick the column that applies for each item.

Negative effects	Experienced?	Used?
Irritants: Certain words in common use can have a negative effect on the opposition. For example, some people repeat a conversation closer such as: 'Know what I mean?' after almost every sentence, or 'To be honest …' which may lead one to think that that is a quality that the speaker definitely does not have.		
Counter-proposals: Trying to 'score' by opposing suggestions for no reason; if used repeatedly, this could lead to conflict		
Defence and attack spirals: Tit-for-tat playground-type behaviour which can escalate towards conflict for no real reason		
Argument dilution: Mixing strong and weak arguments in your proposals, which allows your opponents to attack the same mix but picking off the weakest ones first		
Positive effects		
Behaviour labelling: Labelling your interaction with the class of behaviour about to be used and then saying it; this enhances concentration and listening		
Testing understanding and summarizing: A restatement of a previous comment, e.g. 'So, what you're saying is that the new system will be faster and more efficient…'		
Reflection: 'You're saying that you think that some jobs will have to go in the reorganization?'		
Information seeking: Questions designed to progress the negotiation		
Feelings commentary: Revealing how you are feeling about the meeting and discussion		

The papers exchanged at the close may have to be provisional if either party needs to run the figures back at the business or obtain the full acceptance of the organization in cases where an exceptional concession has been agreed (e.g. extended credit). This indicates a link with the earliest phase of the negotiation – establishing the credibility and authority of your opponent.

At this point, perhaps we should review our original purpose in meeting. There may have been clear requirements for us to achieve a win/win, win/lose or even lose/lose result, and summaries will give both parties the chance to consider whether sufficient progress has been made.

CASE STUDY: EXPLORING A PERFORMANCE PROBLEM

Meeting between Bill Case, BuGS Operations Director, Tim, Area Operations Manager and, later, Tom, driver

Bill: Right, now, what's this all about? I hear that the drivers are angry. One of your jobs is to avoid this kind of disruption! We're a family business and a major part of your job is to keep customer-service people happy – or they upset the customers.

Tim: Yes, you know that these kinds of problems are very rare; but we seem to have a disruptive person in the crew. He's only been at the branch for less than six months and came highly recommended from a local agency.

Bill: Yeah, well … that's another factor. I don't know why we are still using agencies; they are like highway robbers. Perhaps they'll want to find him another job somewhere else and he can be disruptive there! Anyway, what's all this about faking his hours sheet?

Tim: Well, as you know, his branch only has the one driver so, if it had happened here at the main branch, I would have suspended him immediately pending a full enquiry but at Branch 10 we'd then have to get another agency driver and they are scarce and very expensive.

Bill: Look, have you got evidence? If so, just sack him! We don't want any illegality with drivers – and there's always the risk of the gutter press publicizing the fact that we employ fraudsters and tolerate unsafe practices. Just do it!

Tim: That's what this meeting is about! But it's not quite as simple as all that. I hear that this driver is a member of the Drivers' Union and, while none of the other drivers belongs (as far as I know), if we handle his case badly there's a possibility they'll all join up and life will become much more difficult – especially when we want to employ them for overtime in our busiest season.

Bill: Pah! Unions will be the death of this country! Well we'd better see him. Can you fetch him in, now?

Tom: Hiya! My name's Tom and I'm sure it's some kind of mistake that I've been told to come here – I've got days of back deliveries to catch up on.

Bill: What? (*to Tim*) What's that all about?

Tim: I'll talk to you about that later –

Tom: I can answer that. The lorry's been in service bay for several days now, waiting for new parts; unfortunately the service agents you use are cheap but they don't keep parts – so this is what happens!

Bill: (*to Tim*) I'm beginning to regret that I ever got involved in all this… Did you know about it? If so, why am I the last person to know?

Tim: With respect, I did put an email into your office yesterday, but there's little to be done other than hire a replacement temporarily – or order a new lorry, of course. Either way, there's nothing in the budget for that.

Tom: (*under his breath*) What a bunch of cheapskates! No wonder the sales office people are so worried about redundancies!

Bill: Who's said anything about redundancies?

Tim: No, it's not been discussed – but there was some disquiet at a project meeting the other day when the new order system was being discussed. We squashed the rumours, of course. But let me get back to the issue of your hours, Tom.

Tom: Oh, no! Not again!

Tim: There are some inaccuracies with your schedule – and your weekly hours claim shows overtime that doesn't match the records of the lorry and there's one day when the shift exceeds your 'safe hours' limit. Can you explain any of that?

Tom: I did explain it to the Branch Manager but he seemed to be more interested in this new gizmo they're testing – something to do with customer ordering? Don't know what all the fuss is about; people are much more reliable… and if your lorry's off the road, the customer is let down anyway.

Tim: None of that has anything to do with your hours … and I do need you to answer up.

Bill: (*to Tom*) No, don't! I've heard quite enough… you're suspended pending further enquiries into these records. Sounds like we have a potential case of fraudulent records, illegal driving and goodness knows what else!

(*to Tim*) You'd better get another agency driver and vehicle in to cover for a week – allocate the charge to my contingencies budget and report to me tomorrow on the backlog.

(*to Tom*) Leave any other paperwork that you have with Ops before you leave the building – and please keep away from the branch and its customers until all this is cleared up.

Tom: (*leaving*) Don't worry, I'll be pleased to be out of it! I'll leave my keys downstairs. You'll all be sorry for this enormous mistake.

COACHING SESSION 89

Analysing the case study

Problems can occur in all organizations from time to time and in this case the initial enquiry was seeking to get to the facts of what had gone wrong.

1. Did they achieve that? If not, what facts were missing?

2. What was the mood of the meeting?

3. Do you think it was genuine fact-finding discussion or had decisions already been made?

There is a difference between negotiating over facts and suspicions – and uncorroborated evidence rarely helps achieve a win/win result. However, Bill might well feel satisfied that his strong leadership style has straightened out the situation. Tom may have appeared to 'sit on the fence'.

4. Will the situation improve now – or could it get worse? Note down what you think will happen next and what you think *should* happen.

ONLINE RESOURCE

The BuGS meeting

For a practical analysis of the BuGS case, 'Exploring a performance problem', go to:

www.TYCoachbooks.com/Negotiation

Sequenced meetings – or not?

The PROD-ProSC formula of sequenced meetings provides a valuable framework for us to use in 'set-piece' negotiations, but will it always work?

The strange thing about negotiation is that better results are generally obtainable when the players are equally well trained. In other words, one side or the other may gain an advantage but the overall aim should be for a 'quality win' – one that benefits all parties. By reverse argument, the failure to adopt a sequenced approach to the meeting does not necessarily indicate a naive or untrained negotiator. It may point to a deliberate attempt to form an individual style – or to gain some tactical advantage – and, when coupled with the exercise of a charismatic personality, the result can be extraordinarily effective.

Therefore, while the logical approach to the meeting may appear to be the best method to adopt, you should always be alert to unstructured approaches and develop the ability to use or respond to these, too.

THE PROD-ProSC MAP

As before, your current position on the map is highlighted in bold.

Stage	Issues
P = Prepare	
a) People	Who am I meeting? With what authority?
	Who else is likely to be present?
	What do I know about the culture and style of representatives of this business?
b) Place	Where will we meet? Home or away?
	What is the meeting room like?
	How can I make the communications work for me?
	How affected am I likely to be by the personal comfort factors?

Stage	Issues
R = Research	What do we know about the trend of deals in this sector? How might this affect our goals?
	Have I a clear shopping list of objectives and parameters worked out for each one?
	What could be our opponents' position?
	How could I find out in advance?
	Who might have the power in this relationship?
	How could it be used for mutual benefit?
O = Open	How should I open the meeting?
	What ice-breaking topics might be used?
	Are there any probing questions I could ask? How could we establish some common ground?
D = Debate and discuss	What style of conversation should I adopt? Collaborative/consensus/competitive?
	What kind of response is this likely to bring?
Pro = Propose	How will I resist the temptation to move too quickly/slowly?
	How could trial proposals help? How will I ensure that all my proposals are conditional?
Conflict management	What if we disagree in a major way?
S = Summarize and conclude	**How good am I at using summaries in meetings?**
	How will I remember to use summaries during and at the end of the meeting?
	Have we got all the facts we need to close the deal?
C = Close	Who will be responsible for tracking progress at the meeting and at the end?
	How can I ensure that appropriate notes are taken and that they are accurate and complete?
	How strong is my decision-making ability?
	What methods of closing can I use most effectively?
	If my authority is challenged, how will I manage this?
	What are the risks to implementation?

Once you have explored your current stage, note in your action plan any areas that might need more attention.

NEXT STEPS

In this chapter you learned about the important steps you need to take towards summarizing and concluding a deal, taking into account the factors that can hinder the final agreement or cause a loss of momentum.

The next chapter will give you a deeper understanding of the importance of celebrating success, reviewing key skills and tracking progress and milestones, while keeping in mind an understanding of the risks to implementation.

👍 TAKEAWAYS

How clearly do you signal agreement? How do you check that other parties' agreement is secure?

_____

_____

_____

_____

_____

What remedial action have you taken after failures?

_____

_____

_____

_____

How do you use summaries? How could you use them as progress commentaries to encourage movement towards the closing position?

_____

_____

_____

_____

How will you use labelling in future negotiations?

_____

_____

_____

_____

How would you handle your partners' hesitation and reluctance in seeking mutual agreement?

_____

_____

_____

_____

How would you read opponents' behaviours and attitudes and encourage them to move towards your objectives?

_____

_____

_____

_____

List here the actions you will take to improve your results from the content and outcomes of your negotiations:

_____

_____

_____

_____

10 | IMPLEMENTATION AND PROGRESS TRACKING

 OUTCOMES FROM THIS CHAPTER

- Know the risks to implementation.
- Reflect on and review your key skills as a negotiator.
- Know how to track progress and 'milestones'.
- Prevent and deal with problems.
- Understand the importance of celebrating success.

In the closing, the final part of the PRO-ProSC process, you will be discussing how the agreement will be implemented and the ways of tracking progress. To underpin the importance of negotiation as a *practical* process (which should be enhanced by the key skills illustrated in this book – and not the other way round!), this last chapter starts with a final scenario from our main case study. Your challenge is to identify the practical techniques previously discussed that are helping to contribute to, and achieve, a win/win deal. The moral is that, with determination and concentration, a good outcome is the norm and not the exception.

Our mission remains to guide you towards even better results through the key skills illustrated here – but real life is rarely perfect, which is why successful negotiators are, above everything else, essentially practical people. Over-complication is avoided on the basis that 'simple things rarely go wrong'.

CASE STUDY: MEETING BETWEEN BuGS, SUPREME SYSTEMS AND OUZI

Background

A joint pilot project (between BuGS and Supreme) has been launched in order to test out the system and Ouzi laptops, in conjunction with one of the BuGS's smaller, rural branches. This was successful until the last couple of weeks, when data communication methods became unreliable, and this has led to a concerning complaint from a long-established and loyal customer. This is still being investigated by BuGS's IT Manager.

There have also been some organizational changes:

- **At BuGS** there is a new MD, Andy (previously Finance Director) and a new Sales Director, Sandy (from a competitor); Mac, the previous GM (Sales) left when Sandy's appointment was made.

- **At Supreme Systems**, Jan has been promoted to Operations Director.

- **At Ouzi Computers**, Lin has been promoted from Home Sales to General Manager. Billy is on long-term secondment to Ouzi's main factory in South Korea.

Meeting venue: BuGS Boardroom

Present: Andy (MD and Chair); Sandy (Sales Director); Noel (IT Manager)

Visitors: Jan (Operations Director, Supreme); Lin (General Manager, Ouzi Computers)

1. Andy: Welcome to our new Boardroom and I believe that congratulations are in order for Jan – Supreme's new Operations Director and Lin – who I believe has become Ouzi's European General Manager?

2. Jan: Thank you very much – and I note that you have also received a new challenge as head of BuGS.

3. Andy: You could call it that – it feels more like dragging a reluctant donkey kicking and screaming into the twenty-first century – some of the procedures and customs are more akin to the nineteenth century! Now we ought to get down to business – I think I ought to warn you that this is going to be a pretty difficult meeting!

4. Jan: Well, we are eager to please – and see BuGS as an important test of our growing credibility in the construction and distribution industries. Lin and I are here to straighten out the current laptop computer problems and set out our forward plan for a roll-out around your other branches.

5. Andy: I hope you can retain that confidence – we are facing a pretty messy situation! Sandy, can you explain the position, please?

6. Sandy: Right, well, you'll remember that we talked on the phone about the erratic performance of the laptops on test – and wrote a detailed complaint – which, by the way, has never been acknowledged, let alone answered. Noel, do you want to summarize what you found?

7. Noel: As you'll know from our report, I stripped one down and found some non-proprietary components inside; frankly, we were shocked that Ouzi should have tried to get away with such a cost-saving. We had expected much more professionalism and a robustness that would have been guaranteed by a standard assembly and warranty. It's the sort of behaviour that even an undergraduate would not have done!

8. Lin: I agree, but I'm afraid that Ouzi was not to blame for that; it was in complete contravention of all our contracts and performance standards which are signed by our distributor partners – including Supreme.

9. Noel: So what you are saying is that your partner, Supreme, is accountable?

10. Jan: Hang on a minute! Supreme is innocent here! I'll accept that we did try out a simple experiment to speed up the processing of orders – but we never encouraged any of our people to open up any of the computer cases – only to try out a couple of 'dongles'. That was Billy Smart's idea and, as soon as we discovered the effect of what he was trying to do, we parted company with him. I had hoped that would be the end of the matter and that we could move ahead with the roll-out!

11. Andy: Not so fast! Unfortunately, this affair has had worse consequences – isn't that right, Sandy?

12. Sandy: Yup! I'm afraid so, we've had a serious complaint from one of our best clients in the country – an independent builder of social housing who is trusted by the planners – because he is good at speedy completions once planning approval has been given.

To cut a long and very sad story short, he placed a very substantial order for house bricks through Mac (our former GM) who processed the order through the laptop and all trace of it was lost! Needless to say, we knew nothing of the situation until the day came when the bricks were needed – and had a very worried customer on the phone. We were horrified as it meant a 35-day delay for more expensive bricks which had to be express-imported from the Continent.

Understandably, the planners were even angrier, as the local authority missed their 'new-build' targets, which were a major point of political advantage over their local opponents. We're now facing joint legal action by both the Authority and the builder; Mac resigned at once but I don't think he was the only person to blame.

13. Jan: No, I'm afraid you're right – he and Billy were 'drinking pals' and he might have turned a blind eye to some of Billy's little ways! We fired Billy, of course, and his mate, Jimbo, seems to have skipped the country!

14. Andy: Well, I've heard it all now! Do you people not have any controls over the activities of your staff? I think we'd better brief our lawyers!

15. Jan: Let's not be too hasty – the risk is that the negative publicity from court action would punish both of us beyond any agreed compensation. Clearly, we have a lot of apologizing to do and, with the support of our backers and Ouzi, I suggest that we can put things right by exploiting the success of the new system – and roll it out. Once it's fully operational, it really does have the potential to bring you great competitive advantage! What do you think, Lin?

16. Lin: None of us comes out of this unscathed! The ironical thing is that this non-approved modification proved that a small component – that our designers claimed could not work – has the potential to speed up the order processing – and be a market winner. The factory didn't want to accept that anyone else knew better than them – these lads actually did us a favour! (And our Board has paid tribute to the innovation and persistence of BuGS and us in creating this innovation. That'll give your PR people a fantastic story to sell!).

I have the authority of our corporate MD to make financial amends, provided we can agree a roll-out plan with, say, just a two-month period of trouble-free running with the new model. How do you feel about all that?

17. Andy: I like the sound of that – I've never had a great love for lawyers and court cases – they distract from the money-making process! I suggest we take a break for refreshments and reconvene in an hour? Let's see how we could make this work?

18. Lin: That's very kind – do you have a quiet room that we could use to prepare an offer?

19. Andy: Sure – use this room – we'll send in a drinks trolley – my office is next door if you need anything else.

[Break]

20. Andy: Are we ready to reconvene? And would you like to make a start?

21. Lin: Yes. we have an outline plan to offer:

a) Supreme, in partnership with Ouzi International plc, will, without any further acceptance of liability, underwrite compensation for Mr Independent Builder – amount to be agreed with the client in a joint negotiation with BuGS. (Our expectation will be an agreement that is 'in kind' rather than cash.)

b) This is on condition that the whole matter will be closed to any external scrutiny or publicity – until the new computer system is ready to roll out – and then the relaunch will be led solely by Ouzi's World Press Agency (who are renowned for their impact and trust).

How does that sound?

22. Andy: Very interesting – and thank you for your careful deliberations. We, too, have some thoughts on how we would see the future – Noel?

23. Noel: We have considered the position with the 'dongle' and, as it was developed by one of our employees – even though it had some unfortunate side effects – we intend to claim copyright in this product; we started the initial procedures last month. We also invite Supreme/Ouzi to share our new computer training school project – which will be tendering for public contracts part-funded by HM Government – on a 51/49 percentage basis.

24. Lin: You have been busy! You'll understand that I do not have the authority to agree to all that today; however, I need to contact HQ tomorrow and will actively seek their support. Can we reconvene tomorrow afternoon?

25. Andy: Why not? Shall we say 3 p.m.?

(There is a positive 'buzz' as the meeting breaks up.)

RISKS TO IMPLEMENTATION

Remember the saying, 'If it can go wrong, it will!' Greedy negotiators sometimes fail to have their agreements implemented, but never find out why. Only rarely do situations occur when a deal entered into in good faith goes seriously wrong and attempts are made to hide the truth. Mostly, excuses are made for non-implementation that are plausible and unlikely to lead to the other party checking up.

For example, it may be said that:

- 'The business has been taken over.' Does the new management want to make a profit from continuing in this market? If so, how will the takeover affect its policies? When or how will we find out?

- 'You'll need to see my new boss to renegotiate this deal.' Alternatively, you could write direct to Head Office in Japan/America/Korea!

- 'Recent reorganization has changed all our levels of authority and I'm waiting to hear how this will affect my job.'

- 'A fire at the factory destroyed all the stock.' Which factory where? Whose stock? What alternatives exist? How will our lost profit be recouped? What, if any, compensation will be available?

All of these reasons will sound entirely plausible but, when weeks have elapsed for the negotiation process to unfold – with approval negotiated on both sides – should we put the disruption down just to bad luck?

COACH'S TIP

Be persistent in dealing with problems

Unforeseen problems occur all the time in negotiations, but dedicated and persistent negotiators take pride in their ability to extract the plums from the fire. Collaborative relationships extend beyond the tendering and contract drafting process; sometimes negotiators need to help a supplier or client out of real difficulties.

COACHING SESSION 90

Implementing the deal

Contracting the deal is just the start of the project. Its successful implementation is essential if all those 'dreams and wishes' are to be realized.

1. Have you thought about – and worked through – a plan for its implementation? How workable is it?

_____

_____

_____

_____

2. If a plan exists, what essential changes need to be effected – against an agreed time plan – to ensure that the necessary resources are available in time?

_____

_____

_____

_____

_____

_____

_____

3. If no plan exists, how will you produce a critical path analysis plan showing a full 'needs list' – together with time markings indicating when the steps will need to be carried out?

_____

_____

_____

_____

4. Who will be responsible for this? And what will be your input into it?

_____

_____

_____

_____

IMPLEMENTATION FAILURE

Many people can be readily tempted with thoughts of how a large National Lottery win could change their lives. The odds against winning do not seem to stop people playing and so it can be that negotiators fall for this – one of the most dangerous of commercial sins. Greed causes people (who think they have spotted a chance to get rich) to buy or sell all of a product in the hope of dominating the market. However, sudden market changes may lead to desires to cancel/sell to another party (who is now prepared to buy at an even higher premium) and everything may seem fine until the bubble bursts.

Distortions in markets do happen from time to time in all walks of life, but periods of heavy demand usually precede periods of famine and it can take a long time before growth starts again. (A good illustration of this lies with European residential property values, which rose at a phenomenal rate before a substantial crash – resulting in many householders holding negative equity. This situation was unheard of in peacetime and brought a sharp decline in economic activity in all the professions and trades related to house purchase.) Skilled negotiators have a watchful eye and concern for the future, while making the most of immediate opportunities.

COACHING SESSION 91

Reviewing your key skills

All experienced negotiators have their favourite ways of working – and probably like to think that their approach is personal to them and not to be emulated by others: the value of their efforts is seen in their results. Before the contribution to management learning from key business authors and consultants, most of these skills were gained through the trials and tribulations of life; experience was gained through trial and error, reinforced by distinctive results and genuine trust between the players.

1. Choose a partner for this task (preferably someone who is also a negotiator in your organization).
2. There are seven key skills listed and your task is to distribute 20 points over the list – allocating proportions of your votes according to the potential that each statement would have in helping you achieve your objectives. Please do this separately, then get together with your partner and seek to persuade/negotiate with each other to achieve a new agreement.

   A: To give as much attention to planning as conducting the negotiation

   B: To commence negotiation with an extreme demand

   C: To stick with your strategy once you have fixed it

   D: To consider and make allowances for the personal needs of your opponent

   E: To identify winning and losing strategies and avoid being the loser

   F: To make your deadlines quite clear to your opponent

   G: To avoid emotional situations

When you have completed this task, discuss how you arrived at an agreed solution and how the 'give-and-take' worked. You might be surprised just how much give-and-take has occurred – especially if charm has played a part! This exercise should have illustrated how easy it is to use these negotiation skills in an objective way, applying numerical values to principles. Real life utilizes the same principles – but personal (or organizational) priorities tend to dictate negotiators' priorities – in debate, and flexibility depends on delegated freedom to settle within an acceptable band.

TRACKING PROGRESS AND TARGETS

Most complex projects involve sequential activities, which presume prompt availability of:

- products
- services (professional and utilities)
- time
- budgets for incidental/related expense
- appropriate knowledge and skills at all points.

Much can be learned from the role of site management professionals who rely on the application of critical path management principles to ensure that orderly progress is made. Diagrammatic charts and committed deadline dates are essential for a disciplined approach – but this is not the total answer.

The real negotiation need arises if or when the plan slips or goes wrong because of some unpredicted crisis which threatens a serious delay. This is when favours are called in and loyalty is tested. This is negotiating within the constraints of the possible – and negotiators who are successful in keeping the process going – are worth their weight in gold, around the world. Such people speak with confidence and assurance and have a widely appreciated reputation for resolving problems. This is reassuring for all concerned – but it comes at a cost.

The key is effective communication, which means paying attention to:

- use of language to match the situation and the needs of the other party
- keeping objectives always in mind
- clarity of intention and meaning
- obtaining feedback.

COACHING SESSION 92

Your custom and practice checklist

Ask yourself these questions about custom and practice in negotiating, to help with your action plan. Tick the box that applies to you.

Custom and practice	OK	Need help
Have we negotiated on these issues before?		
Are there any precedents? (If not, why make one now?)		
Are our opponents seeking to renegotiate an existing agreement? If so, why? (What is our historical stance on this?)		
Is the purpose of a renegotiation to tighten up the working of an existing agreement?		
If so, has there been any unilateral attempt to impose a full agreement against convention (i.e. working to rule)?		
Do we have a typical timescale for settlement of negotiations?		
Does this provide a framework for future negotiations?		
Is there a commitment to it on both sides?		
Have we honoured it?		

1. What experiences have you had, historically, which support these custom and practice issues?

_____

_____

_____

_____

2. Who holds back-records that could provide additional briefing?

_____

3. Your action plan:

_____

_____

_____

_____

☺☺ COACHING SESSION 93

Your planning checklist

Ask yourself these questions about your progress in planning, to help with your action plan. Tick the box that applies to you.

Planning	OK	Need help
Have we established our most and least favourable positions?		
How far are we prepared to move from our starting position?		
Have we prepared a strategy for obtaining movement?		
Can we link any issues?		
How can we use hypothetical argument (e.g. 'Supposing...')?		
Have we prepared an adjournment strategy?		
Can sanctions be applied as part of the bargaining process?		
How do the parties view the need to bargain fairly?		
Have trust and integrity been built up by: ■ not withdrawing an unconditional offer once it is made? ■ not denying a facility/offer when it has been previously unambiguously accepted? ■ not appealing to the opposition direct until after negotiation has failed?		
Have we demonstrated a willingness to bargain on any issue that has been accepted as negotiable?		
Have we used only information declared formally or publicly in achieving a formal commitment?		
Have we ensured that opponents do not lose credibility in the eyes of their team?		
Have we ensured that there is no trickery in the final agreement?		
Have we ensured that the final bargain is implemented in that form?		
Does our negotiation case have a central theme? For example: ■ Periodic increase ■ Profitability ■ Adjustment of distortions ■ Trust and goodwill ■ Exploitation of bargaining power ■ Maintenance of status quo ■ Effort/reward ratio ■ National interest ■ Good employer/ee ■ Parity and differential ■ International comparison		

1. What experiences have you had, historically, which support these planning issues?

_____

_____

_____

_____

_____

_____

2. Your action plan:

_____

_____

_____

_____

_____

_____

🗩🗩 COACHING SESSION 94

Your debating checklist

Ask yourself these questions about your progress in debating, to help with your action plan. Tick the box that applies to you.

Clarifying opponents' position	OK	Need help
Do we make use of: ■ judging the climate through informal meetings? ■ the 'chance' remark at, or after, a meeting on a different subject? ■ the grapevine? ■ thinking yourself into their shoes? ■ playing devil's advocate? ■ persistently seeking clarification of the opponent's position?		

Changing the expectations of the opponent – undermining their arguments		
Could we: ■ question the assumptions on which argument is based? ■ question the basic facts? ■ question the conclusions? ■ question why they omitted certain related issues? ■ amplify the weakness in the argument? ■ suggest the need for revision (when we suspect they no longer believe in their case)? ■ project consequences if such an argument were implemented (these must be dramatic but not absurd)? ■ paint the (emotional) picture of the consequences (e.g. short-time, no money, cancelled holidays, disappointed families)?		
Undermining credibility of our opponent		
Could we: ■ attack the negotiator's self-confidence? ■ refer their argument back – inferring that they are out of touch with people/situation? ■ refer the argument back to their superiors? ■ refer to their lack of age/experience? ■ compare them unfavourably with their predecessors? ■ compare their ideas unfavourably with person(s) they are known to respect? ■ work on to the point that our opponent experiences mental exhaustion?		
Enhancing own arguments and credibility		
Do we ever: ■ highlight our own strengths by emphasizing assets, mastery, benefits to them, reasonableness, emotional appeal, no equivocation? ■ minimize weaknesses? ■ present conversational topics to support our case? ■ build up new demands?		

1. What experiences have you had, historically, which support these debate issues?

_____

_____

_____

2. Your action plan:

COACHING SESSION 95

Your proposing and bargaining checklist

Ask yourself these questions about your progress in proposing and bargaining, to help with your action plan. Tick the box that applies to you.

Propose and bargain: obtaining movement	OK	Need help
How do we use tactics to encourage movement?		
Reading the signs of the movement for real business?		
The summary of progress so far?		
Trial proposal – to test willingness to move?		
If…then?		
Linking issues?		
The adjournments?		
Our 'sprat'…their 'mackerel'?		
Building on a friendly ally in the opponent's team?		
Appeal to their better nature?		
Putting on pressure – e.g. time deadlines, mental exhaustion?		
How do we encourage a reduction in their commitment?		
Emphasizing their 'generous' movement to help them save face?		
Relating their movement to 'changed circumstances'?		
Blaming a popular (external) scapegoat?		

Encouraging a movement as a result of a 'misunderstanding'?		
Changing the negotiators to break deadlock?		
Erecting a smokescreen to cover loss of face (e.g. a thick report)?		
Making the opponent feel better by being understanding?		
Do we ever: ■ make the offer public to emphasize it is final? ■ confirm the offer in writing? ■ try to get agreement now to avoid more meetings, etc? ■ use the walk-out? ■ use sanctions to strengthen the opponents' commitment? ■ use an extra minor inducement for agreement now? ■ use the assumed agreement close? ■ do a deal by 'splitting the difference'? ■ use the 'one last point/objection' close?		

1. What experiences have you had, historically, which support these 'propose and bargain' issues?

_____

_____

_____

_____

_____

2. Your action plan:

_____

_____

_____

_____

_____

PREVENTING PROBLEMS

The unfortunate fact is that many deals do go wrong – for predictable as well as unforeseeable reasons. Some people seem to spend most of their time negotiating their way out of one set of difficulties and straight into the arms of another set! The implementation of an agreement is the most important part of the whole process and the range of possible things that might go wrong at this stage could be the subject of a whole other book. Bloomers exist in every walk of life and organization, but every negotiator will wish that their name is not attached to any of them.

♟♟ COACHING SESSION 96

Negotiating rearguard actions

Answer the following questions about your ability to deal with problems.

Dealing with problems	Yes	Need help
Do I deal with problems well?		
Does sorting out problems/crises make me feel good?		
If the same problems arise again and again, can I work out whether they are self-made or predictable?		
Am I developing a reputation as a fixer (or are people secretly amused/ irritated and calling me a 'busy fool')?		
Is crisis management designed into the job I do? If so, can I influence other people to find better ways of using time and resources?		
If I want to use my resources to better effect, am I applying the lessons of this text as thoroughly as I ought?		
If this would be difficult for me to achieve, working on my own, do I know whose help and support I could enlist?		

When you have considered these issues, compare them with the responses of another negotiator in your organization (perhaps your manager and a negotiator from a different discipline). Consider to what extent 'rearguard negotiating' is endemic in your roles and/or the nature of your organization (and the market itself). Could there be a better way?

_____

_____

_____

_____

To protect ourselves against failure to implement, we need to have the following:

- Accurate and detailed notes/agreed summaries
- Definitions of who will do what to/for whom and for what benefit or cost
- An prepared analysis of what might go wrong at this stage (the 'What if?' question)
- An agreement that is enforceable

Using notes and summaries

With laptops and notepads so readily at hand, there should be no reason why each negotiator should not take a detailed set of notes at each meeting. Unfortunately, it is quite common that we hear one thing at a meeting but write down something else. Mostly this is through 'wishful thinking' or perhaps faulty listening – but how are such discrepancies viewed on the other side when they are eventually discovered? There is no quicker way of leading others to suspect your intentions, or even your integrity.

In some circles, a buyer will insist on an exchange of notes before a representative leaves the buying room and these documents will probably form the basis of the ultimate order placed. Even in such cases, the choices may be difficult to recall after the interview/show or trade mission, so material samples are sought – and maybe Polaroid photographs taken. In very wide-ranging plans or technical specs, it can be difficult to recall, some weeks later, the precise colour or style of an item, which may just be identified on the order form by a product code.

 COACH'S TIP

Record the facts in detail

If a product is delivered and fails to match the sample, you can make a clearer case for a credit if all the facts have been recorded.

Defining terms

Rarely are recordings made of negotiation meetings (if they are, that would indicate a real lack of trust). However, the language used in the meeting may well turn out to be ambiguous when it comes to implementation. Disputes often occur at later dates about 'who said what to whom'.

To avoid this, avoid using vague phrases such as:

- 'as soon as possible' – when, exactly?

- 'the usual size or scale' – whose? Ours, yours or someone else's?

- 'in the popular colours' – whose interpretation of 'popular'? And would this be local, regional, national or international?

It is amazing just how many specification issues are overlooked in commercial negotiating – especially where a price-sensitive market is involved. For example, building blocks may well be available at a substantial discount from someone other than the regular supplier. But do they do the same job? Is their insulation value the same? Maybe not; but the buyer might not care. Some months later the new house owner is wondering why his heating bills are so high and, if moved to investigate, may discover the truth.

The 'What if?' question

- What if there is a docks strike and you cannot obtain the product when you need it? Have you covered yourselves against consequential loss and would there be alternative supply points in such situations?

- What if there are substantial foreign exchange fluctuations and the currency markets move strongly against imported goods and services? Will you still be able to sell these products at a premium?

- What else could go wrong?

Obviously, too many concerns of this type could provide serious disincentives to the deal being made at all. However, some contingency planning should be considered – and maybe some protection built into the contract (or covered by insurance). The last step would probably be to go to court over some consequential loss – but, without a clause in the contract, the negotiator may not even have his or her telephone or fax messages acknowledged (let alone answered).

 COACH'S TIP

Understand expectations

Failure to pay attention to the expectations of the other party can result in the loss of an important deal.

Enforceability

We have all heard of negotiators who thought they had a contract nicely tied up, only to discover that some vital element was missing. Plain contracts are always preferable as disputes are usually simpler to negotiate than complex ones. Ultimately, if both sides wish to continue to work together, then negotiating a mutually acceptable solution to a dispute will be much easier without a huge entourage of specialists, accountants, lawyers, etc. However, the bigger the issue (and sums involved), the more likely it is that the negotiators will need professional support and advice and, in such circumstances, progress may be tediously slow.

 COACH'S TIP

Learn from mistakes

We all make mistakes but the worst mistake of all is to keep making the same ones. By learning lessons from our previous errors, we are more likely to avoid future mistakes in the delicate closing stages of the negotiation meeting. Sadly, too many negotiators learn these lessons the hard way.

One of the objectives of the UK's Industrial Relations legislation in the 1980s was to make IR agreements more enforceable. The problem with this is that trade unions are democratic organizations – they cannot impose a view upon the membership, still less 'police' the agreement. Disputes do arise in which negotiated agreements between management and union representatives are then disowned by the members themselves. Negotiation needs to involve elements of persuasion as well and every manager has found (sometimes to his or her cost) that it is as important to negotiate a deal inside the organization as it is outside. However, some participants on seminars recount with horror how much more difficult internal negotiations actually are than external ones. Negotiation, unfortunately, often gets mixed up with issues of authority, accountability and politics.

Similarly, we can all recount tales of powerful organizations that have (mis)used their power to obtain an unusually advantageous deal from an opponent – only to discover later that it was unenforceable because the other party had gone into liquidation. What price enforceability now?

Negotiation is all about persuading opponents to move from *their* position *towards yours* (as illustrated in the case study). We have seen that this is helped or hindered by the approach and methods we use in the meeting. We can use positive behaviours to improve our success, while negative behaviours are to be avoided.

COACHING SESSION 97

Understanding behaviour and attitudes

Use the following tables to assess both the strengths and the weaknesses of your approach, rating yourself on this scale:

D = I am only just aware of this – I may use it unwittingly
C = I am aware of the technique – I use it occasionally
B = I practise it regularly
A = I use it as often as I can

Positive behaviours	Rating
1. **Behaviour labelling**: indicating the class of behaviour you are about to use (e.g. 'To summarize...')	
2. **Testing understanding and summarizing**: consolidating how the negotiation is going (e.g. 'So, as I understand it...') to clarify/confirm your understanding of what has just been said	
3. **Reflection**: usually repeating a statement in the form of a question (e.g: 'You'd like to have this in writing?')	
4. **Information seeking**: questioning to gain the necessary information to carry on with the negotiation	
5. **Feelings commentary:** letting your opposite number know how you are feeling (e.g. about the meeting or the proposals)	
Negative behaviours	Rating
6. **Irritants:** using words that will have a negative effect on the opposition (e.g. 'rip-off' 'cowboys' 'lunatics' and worse)	
7. **Counter-proposals:** trying to score points by making opposing suggestions	
8. **Defence and attack spirals:** causing conflict for no reason	
9. **Argument dilution:** trying for the lowest common denominator of a series of arguments advanced to support a negotiating position	

Your action plan for promoting the positives and eradicating the negatives:

_____

_____

_____

_____

_____

CELEBRATING SUCCESS

As negotiators, we need to commit to a vital resolution: to 'keep on growing'. Regular negotiators – practising their skills most days – and progressing those deals on a daily, weekly and monthly basis, do not think of this as unusual. It is in thinking about what we are doing – what works well and what needs improvement – that progress can be made.

Some people may view business as drudgery, but the opportunity it presents to make and progress deals can make it full of vitality and creativity. The idea that just one product range, service offer or even entertainment will forever earn us a living is totally unreal in the modern world. While some current 'offers' might be resurrected after a period, the search for creative ways of making a profit provides a great target for our energies and inventiveness. And never have there been such ready-made ways of starting a new venture and/or reinventing or relaunching a business. At the heart of all this activity lies the process of deal making.

Many obstacles can hold us back, and by knowing what they are we can keep on the straight road that will help maintain our progress and lead to success. All organizations need to promote themselves and building good news stories is important, because success breeds success. Creating a public-relations event involving a formal signing of contracts for a merger, a new business, product/ service development or an entertainment would appear to be a natural way of progressing and promoting a business.

Arranging a reception and launch may seem an obvious (if potentially expensive) way of fulfilling the need to celebrate (with or without public-relations specialist support) and it might seem attractive to provide a public signing ceremony. There are some inherent risks in such a plan, however – especially if the signing really is the 'last closure of the deal'. This strategy is sometimes known as 'quivering pen' because it might create considerable discomfort – with the media witnessing the embarrassment. When the good news of the deal has already been announced – or leaked – it places the parties involved in the agreement at risk of one or more of them declaring last-minute needs or stumbling blocks. The pressure is then on to regain the agreement, almost regardless of cost. (In the meantime, all the guests are sampling the champagne and canapés, only becoming aware of the delay as the hours pass.)

COACH'S TIP

Beware of public launches

Public launches and celebrations of deals are probably not a good idea unless all the parties involved can be persuaded not to raise problems on the day – and unless the professional services of a PR company are retained to manage the event.

◯◯ COACHING SESSION 98

Choosing how to celebrate success

With all the effort that will have been invested in a sizeable deal, it is very tempting to plan a celebration to mark the event. However, this should be approached very carefully if the risks are not to outweigh the apparent advantages. Objectives for just a 'public signing' could easily go wrong – and, with the inevitable press occasion, the PR outcome could be disastrous! The risks and benefits do need to be carefully balanced – could this be why so few contract winners conduct these public events?

If the event works well, is it likely to draw more clients or suppliers along to join in?

1. List here the objectives and advantages of a public-relations event:

   _____

   _____

   _____

2. List here the risks of a public relations event:

   _____

   _____

   _____

3. Weigh these against the advantages and objectives of an internal staff celebration:

   _____

   _____

   _____

4. How could you ensure that the client or supplier benefits from the feelings of success that would come from a winning agreement – and in a way that would not cost a fortune (and risk looking as if they are paying for it through the contract)?

   _____

   _____

5. What experiences do you have of a successful promotional event of this kind? And how was it controlled to be risk-free?

COACHING SESSION 99

Reviewing your key planning skills

1. How robust are the skills resources in the team(s) that will implement the plan?

2. How adequately will they cover the demands for the duration of the project(s)?

3. What contingency plan exists to provide alternative resourcing should the team be hit with labour turnover and resulting skills shortages?

4. Who has an input into this element of the plan (e.g. HR and training managers)?

5. What has resulted from such consultation?

COACHING SESSION 100

Tracking progress and milestones

1. Who will monitor progress against milestone indicators and report to managers and team leaders?

2. Who will take management ownership of the project and team-lead it towards a successful completion?

THE PROD-ProSC MAP

As before, your current position on the map is highlighted in bold.

Stage	Issues
P = Prepare	
a) People	What do I know now about the culture and style of representatives of this organization? Are any updates available?
	Does it have the potential to become a 'lasting partner'?
	What level of trust exists between us?
	Who are our contacts? With what levels of authority? How do they treat us? With care? concern? value?...
b) Place	Does the meeting location change the feel/fabric/results? (home/away/neutral)
	How affected am I by the personal comfort factors?
	Am I able to control the communications methods adequately?
	Does the usual location work for both sides (i.e. time/travel needs)?
R = Research	What do we know about the trend of deals in this sector?
	How might this affect our/their goals?
	Have I a clear shopping list of objectives and parameters?
	Do we know our opponents' position?
	How could I find out in advance? Who has the real power in this relationship?
	How well is it being used for mutual benefit?
O = Open	Have we an agreed agenda?
	What probing questions should I ask that might uncover underlying needs and concerns?
D = Debate and discuss	Which style of conversation is most effective with my contact (collaborative/consensus/competitive)?
	What is their normal response?
	How are we able to co-operate but maintain our independence?
Pro = Propose	How can I polish my persuasion skills?
	How will I ensure that all my proposals are conditional?
	How will I set/agree the most effective pace (given the agenda)?
	How will I maintain my concentration and listening skills?
Conflict management	What if we disagree in a major way?

Stage	Issues
S = Summarize and conclude	How will I remember to use progress summaries during and at the end of the meeting?
C = Close	**How will we track progress during the meeting and at the end?**
	How can we ensure that accurate and complete notes are taken?
	How strong is my decision-making ability?
	What methods of closing the deal have we used most effectively?
	Could issues of my own authority be raised or challenged?
	How can we avoid implementation failure?

Once you have explored this final stage, note in your action plan any areas that might need more attention.

ONLINE RESOURCE

The final meeting

See the online resources for the continuation of the case study to the final meeting between the parties, some more tips and reminders of what makes a top negotiator, and a handy checklist for you to use when attending a negotiation as an observer. Go to:

www.TYCoachbooks.com/Negotiation

NEXT STEPS

Now that you have come to the end of the book, you can review your plans for future training. In your action plan, note down the objectives that you would like to achieve over the next 12 months, along with measures of success and timescales. If there is likely to be an large increase in your need for negotiating skills, note down what proportion of your work time is likely to be spent in planning, conducting and/or reviewing negotiations. Introduce changes slowly and carefully, and talk to experienced negotiators. Major change suggests that you may need some performance coaching using CCTV exercises. Again, note what changes may be needed in your personal action plan in the appendix and evaluate all actions.

TAKEAWAYS

Review the questions from the end of Chapter 1.

What are *your* greatest needs in preparing for negotiation meetings?

_____

_____

_____

_____

_____

_____

_____

How much time can you invest in such preparation:

At work?

_____

_____

At home?

_____

_____

How would you like that balance to change (if at all)?

_____

_____

_____

_____

_____

_____

What personal strengths have you identified while reflecting on the ideas in this book?

_____

_____

_____

_____

What progress have you made in identifying and overcoming your 'weak areas'?

_____

_____

_____

_____

What steps will you take in continuing to apply the lessons of this book?

_____

_____

_____

_____

Which style of negotiation are you most comfortable using? And how comfortable are you in handling other styles?

_____

_____

_____

_____

_____

FURTHER READING

Berne, E., *Games People Play* (London: Penguin, 2010)

Cormack, D., *Peacing Together: From conflict to reconciliation* (Monarch, 1989)

Fleming, P., *Negotiate Even Better Deals In A Week* (London: Hodder & Stoughton, 2014)

Fleming, P., *Retail Management* (Management Books, 2004)

Harris, T. A., *I'm OK, You're OK: Climb out of the cellar of your mind* (London: Arrow, 1995)

Hertz, N., *Eyes Wide Open: How to Make Smart Decisions in a Confusing World* (London: William Collins, 2013) (especially 'Step 4 – Ditch Deference and Challenge Experts', 'Step 5 – Learn from Shepherds and Shop Assistants' and 'Step 6 – Overcome your maths anxiety')

Hodgson, J., *Thinking on Your Feet in Negotiations* (London: Pitman, 1994)

Page, R., *Hope Is Not A Strategy: The 6 Keys to Winning the Complex Sale* (New York: McGraw-Hill, 2002)

APPENDIX

YOUR PERSONAL ACTION PLAN

My long-term goal	
Short- and medium-term goals to achieving long-term goal	
Actions required	

Constraints	
Who or what can help me	
Target date for action	

INDEX